MIKE HOFFMAN'S
LOST ART
FOSSILS OF THE FLOPPY AGE
1997-2000

I0478515

Mike Hoffman's LOST ART Fossils of the Floppy Age is published by Mike Hoffman via Hoffman International, 4461 N. Woodburn, Shorewood WI, 53211-1557. All contents are copyright via their respective copyright holders, all materials here are presented for the purpose of scholarly analysis only. No portion of this publication's unique design may be reproduced in any form, by print or electronically, without written permission from the publisher except for review purposes. Additional copies may be obtained from www.mikehoffman.com Wholesale inquiries are welcome. All submissions and letters become property of the publisher. Printed in the United States of America.

An Antique Land...

The dedicated Archaeologist pursues past *objects d'art* with shovels, picks, and finally delicate brushes to gently move away the dust of centuries. No such care was needed in the case of the approximately 350 old "floppy" disks that I used to store artwork on starting way back in 1997 and continuing into 2000. The boxes appeared recently, as if by magic; they'd been stored safely away in the Californian Hoffman International warehouse.

1997 was a long time ago, and it was a very different world, even though just a dozen or so years away from now. The Personal Computer had just appeared, and the Internet was in its infancy. So was Photoshop, with its ancient "glass lens soft" effect, and scanner technology was equally primitive.

Sure, we laugh at Floppy Disk technology today, just as ours will be laughed at ten years hence.

And I was still pursuing publishers back then, so it never occured to me to scan at higher resolutions needed for reproduction. All that technology was still like Voodoo or Black Magic to me.

I was also casting about for ways to make a living as an artist, and my sole plan was to attend comic book conventions all across the country and try to make contacts with collectors. Luckily, the advent of the Internet stopped all that. In fact, I made so many connections online back then that the names (in the form of file names on the floppies) spark foggy remembrances even today.

At some point on some lost afternoon when heading out to the local Flea Market in search of Frazetta-covered paperbacks, I realized that there was just not enough of the stuff out there to satisfy an appetite. What I did then and there was decided to make more on my own--literally, to entertain myself.

But those of you who've followed my work from far enough back know what it was like then, and the price I paid for my Promethean daring. It's all so dull, today.

You may also remember my first art books, *Sorceress* 1 and 2, published by SQP, my first solo comics featuring *Tigress*, my card sets and auctions and all the rest.

This is where we start the journey backwards...

Mike Hoffman 2010

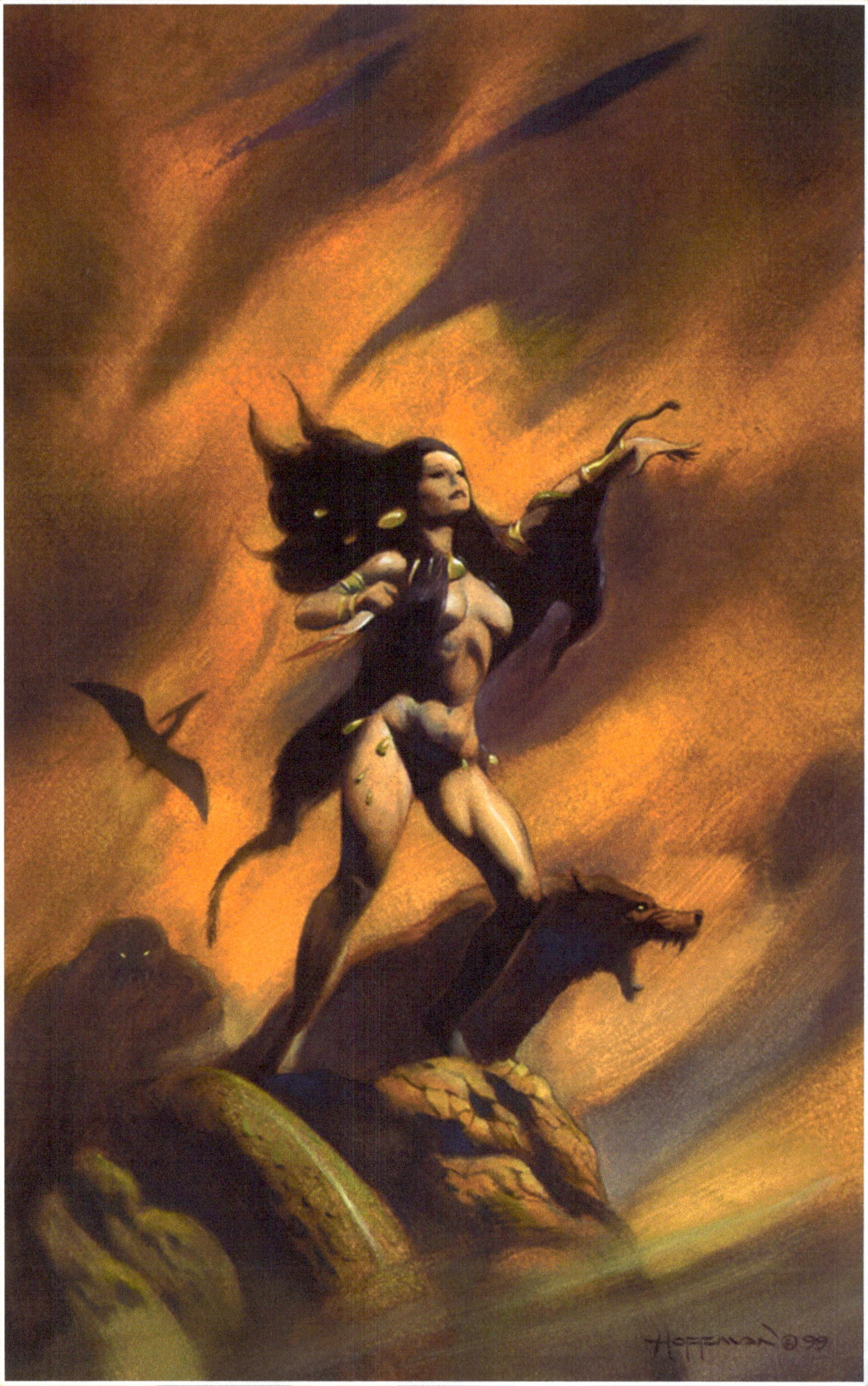

"Witch", a considered cover to the first "Sorceress" art book, oil on Illustration board.

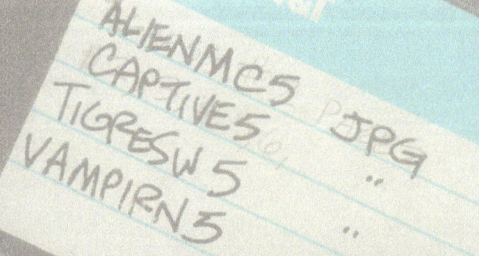

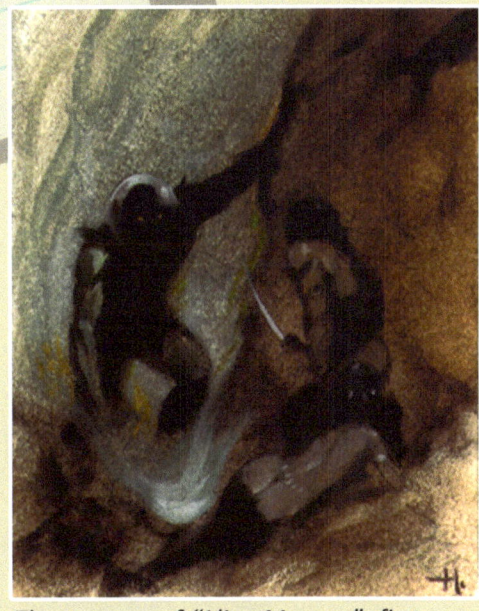 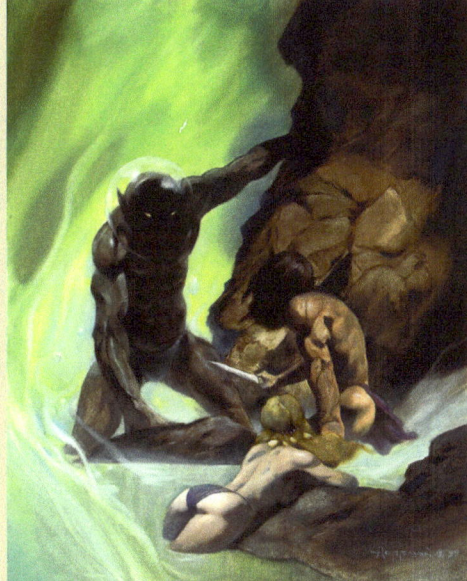 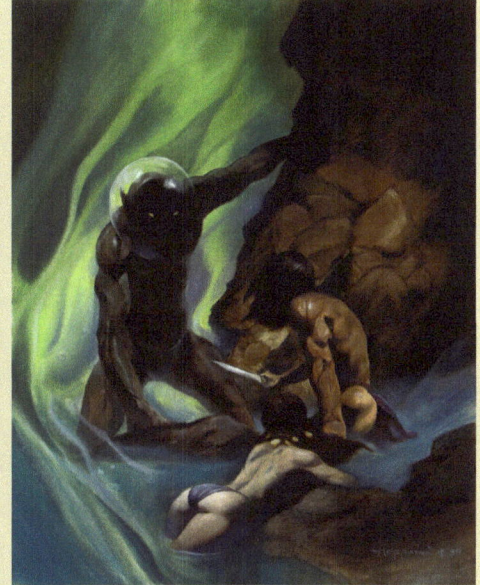

Three stages of "Alien Menace"; first a small oil rough on heavy board, then a first "blond girl" session and a final, finished work.

Looking back at the early artworks I'm amazed at how successful some of them were in spite of the fact I barely knew what I was doing technique-wise.

I think now that the mere fact that I *thought* I could do it counted for a lot, or in other words, *I didn't know I couldn't do it.*

Today it's different--there are doubts hanging all over everything all the time. Doubts, second-guessing, over-thinking, over-planning--it's hard to get back to that raw, unbridled enthusiasm from the early days.

Which is a big part of the "why" of this book.

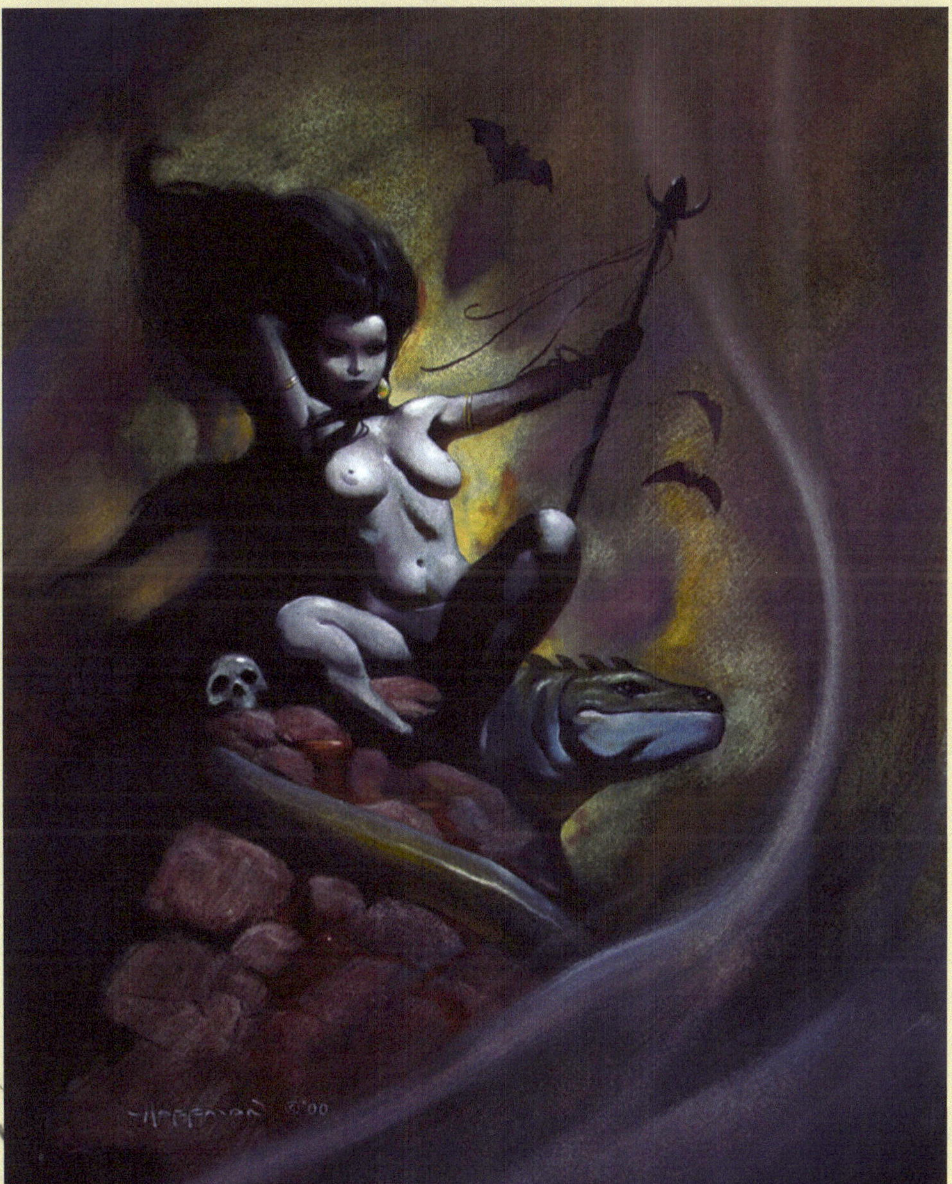

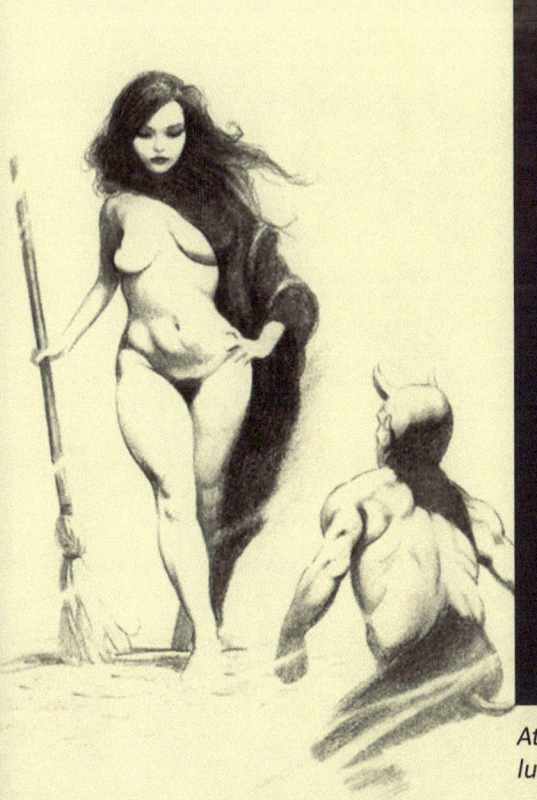

At left: "Witch and Demon", 1997, pencil on paper; Above: "Witches' Peak", oil on illustration board, a painting which I recorded my processes on long-lost video tape.

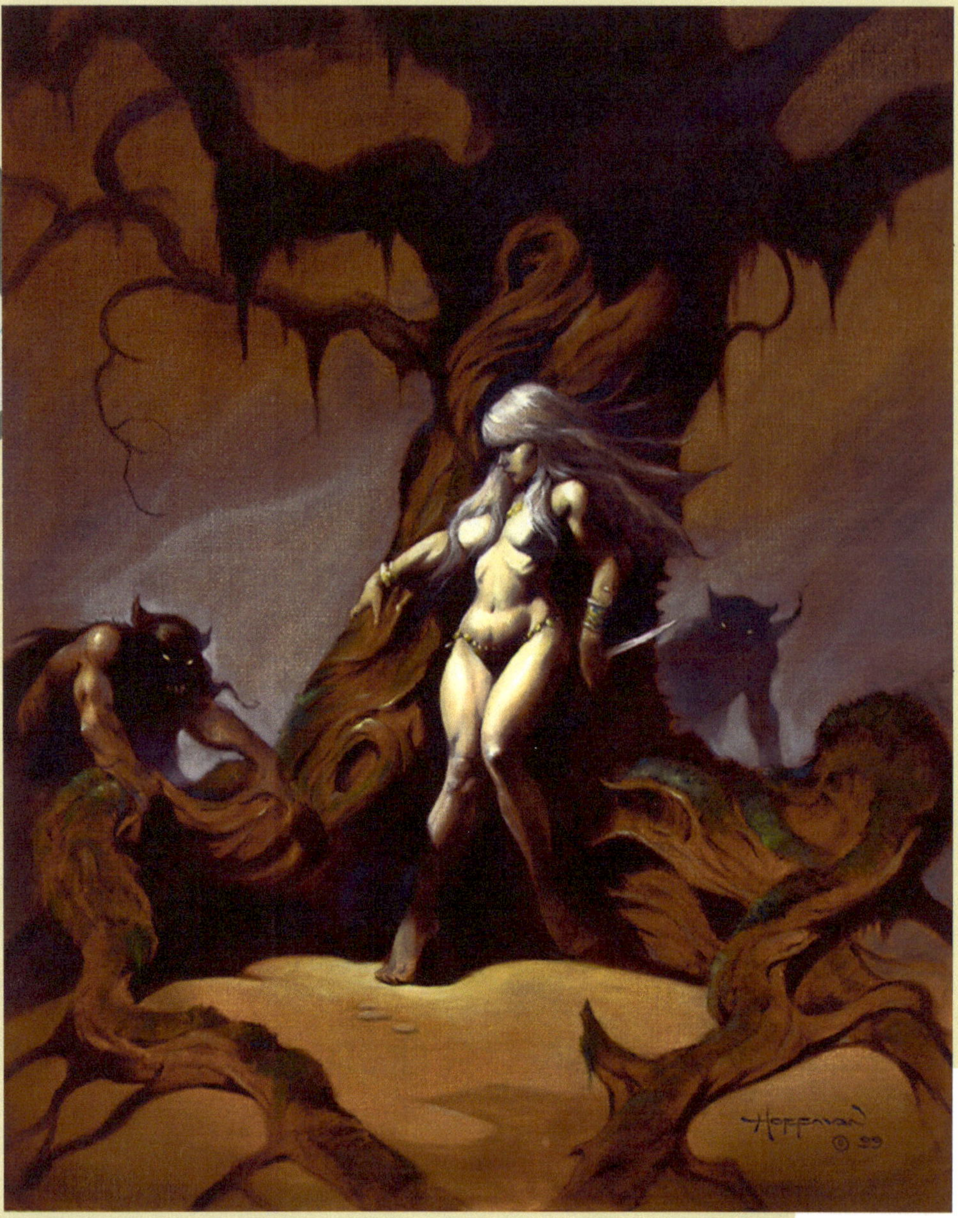

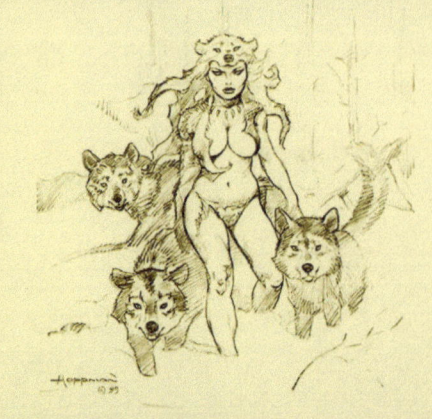

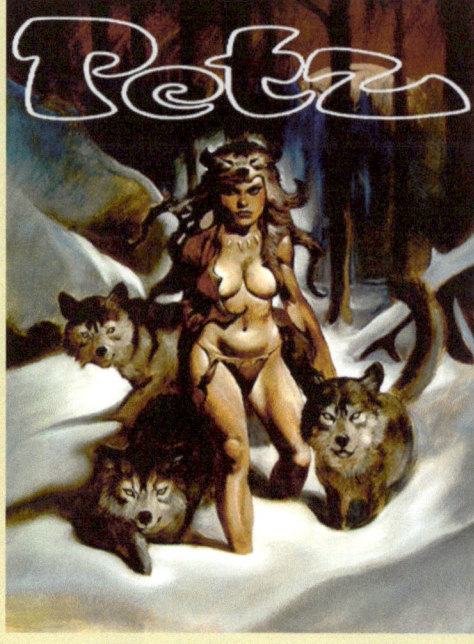

Above: "Wolfmen", painted for a magazine editor's private collection; right: a proposed cover design and sketches for an SQP art book, logo by the artist.

I was big on method back then, and I did a lot of preliminary roughs for paintings, and complex umber underpaintings also. What I didn't know about anatomy or light or color didn't stop me, for I plunged ahead anyway, often blindly. I said to friends at the time that I felt I was being paid to practice, which was essentially true.

In times gone by, I might have been taken on as an apprentice by some old master artist, but of course there were none available in Columbia, South Carolina at the time.

In fact, I did a of of other work, unrelated to Fantasy Art, in order to make ends meet for my fledgling family, like regular commercial assignments for advertising agencies and businesses. I created "standees" for restaurant tables, murals, t-shirts, and countless other artworks.

In fact, I once made an ink drawing of a motor boat for a company for only $25, and it appeared over and over again, gigantically, on billboards all over the city for year afterwards. That sort of robbery is common in commercial and advertising art.

I also designed all the promotional artworks for a very strange company that was just starting out; they intended to combine a hair salon with a skateboard store, where kids could hang out while their moms got preened. "It's a whole new concept" I was told.

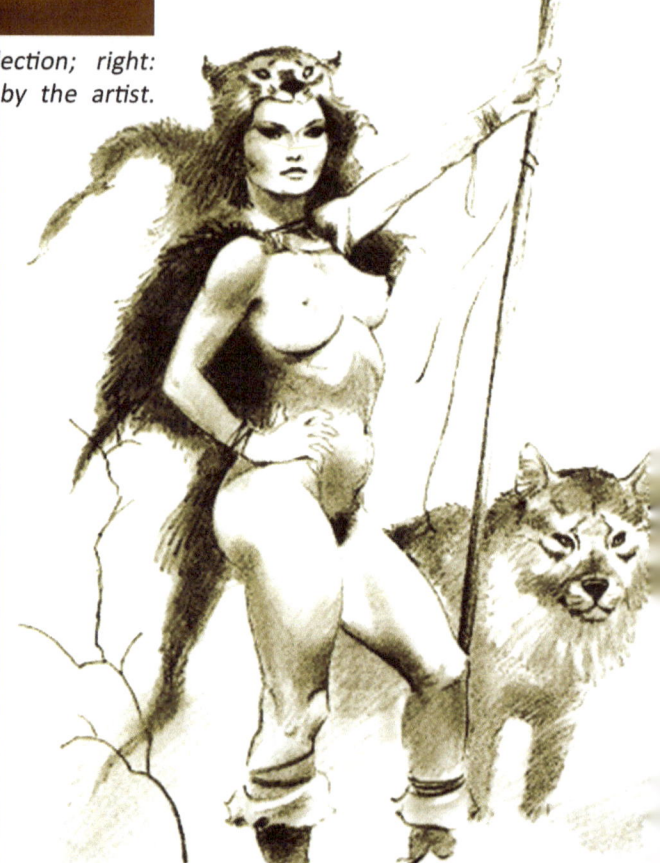

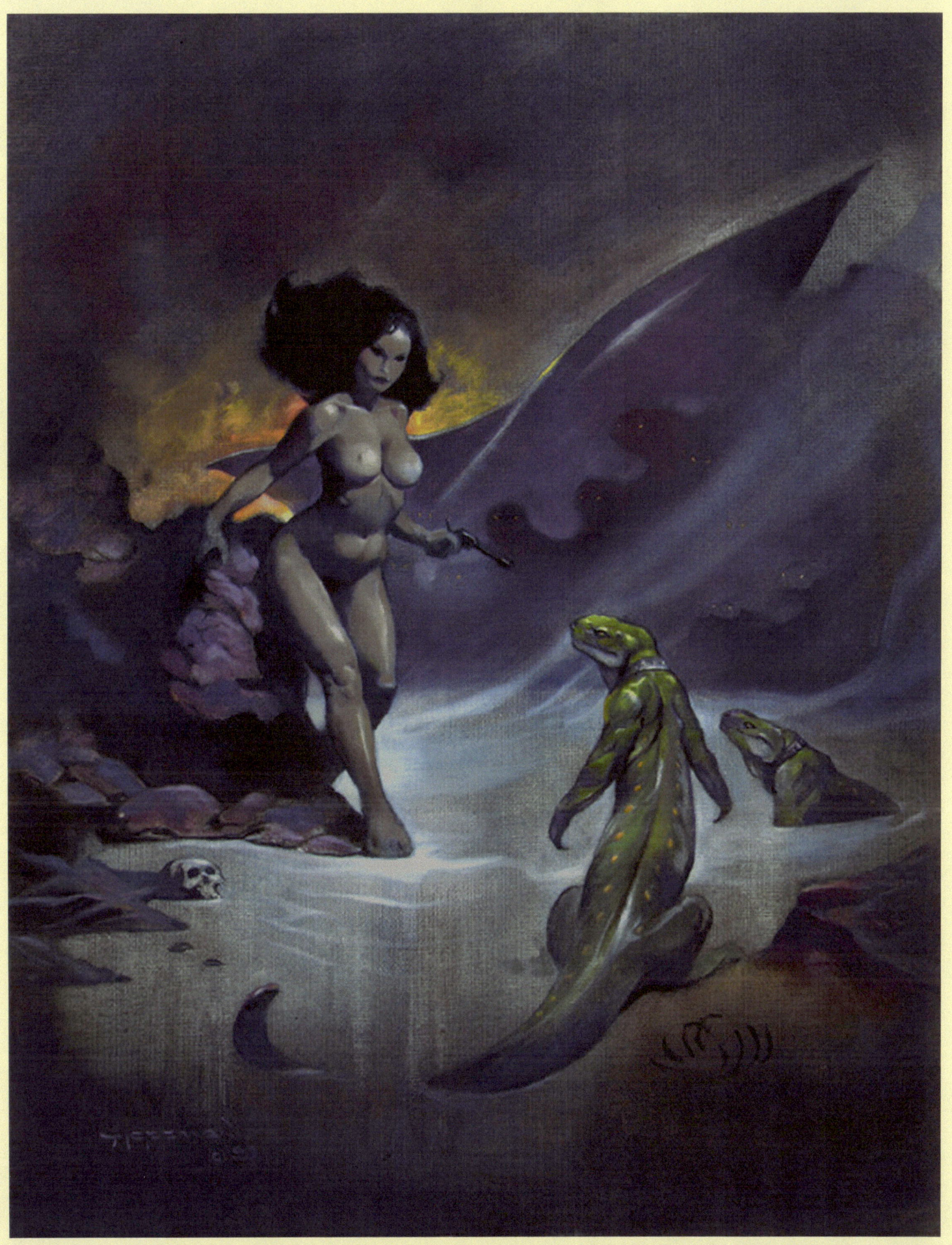

An alien panet is the strange setting for a mysteriously nude astronaut in "Castaway Girl", an early oil painting circa 1999.

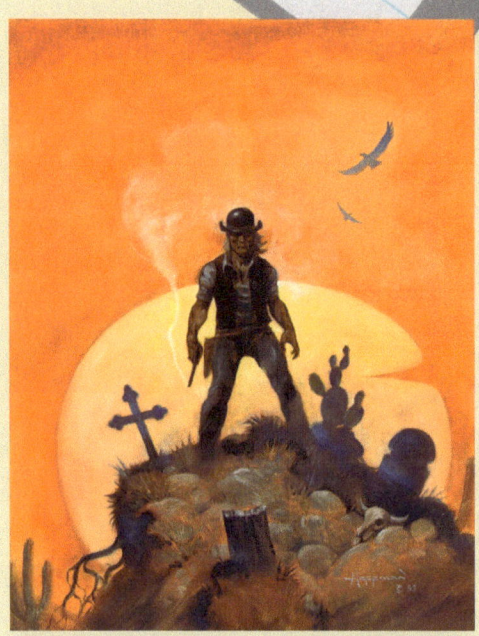
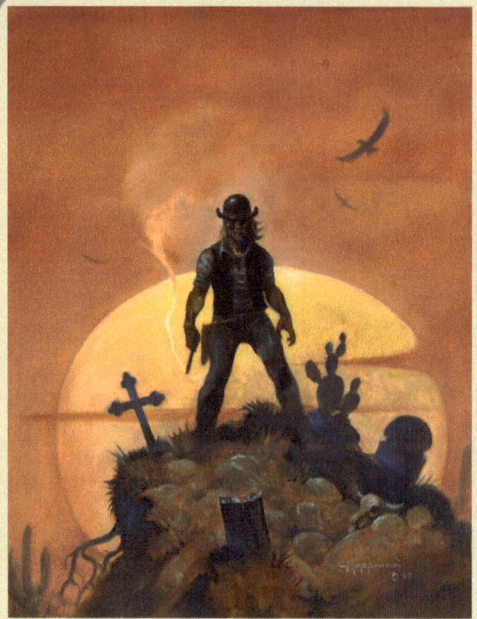
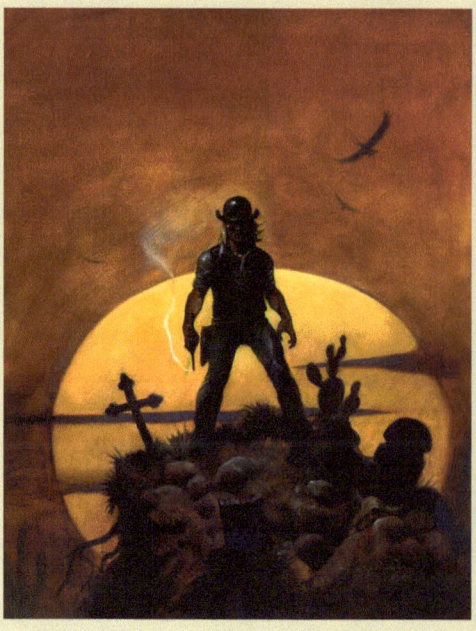

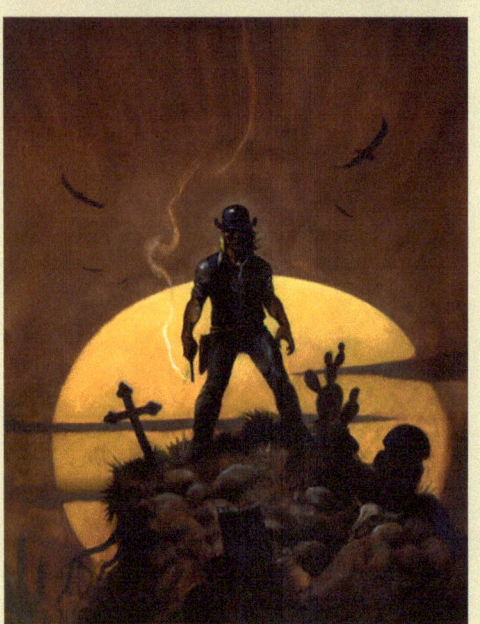

Often I would be caught in the position of not having adequate technical knowledge about Painting, and therefore would "force" the paintings into shape by staring at them endlessly and determining what improvements should be made almost by sheer will-power alone. If that is "training the eye", which I believe it is, then it is training it to exhaustion and failure, which is just as injurious to the acuity of the mind just as it is to the body of an athlete when he overtrains a muscle.

The paintings on this page are cover illustrations for the comic book series *The Ballad of Utopia*, penned by artist and writer Barry Buchanan, whom I met at a comic convention when entering a phase of interest in the Old West and found I had something in common with, in addition to moving torwards being an independent publisher, which he was already.

Above are various versions of the first *BOU* issue's cover art, and there are later, more polished versions than these. Below is a later cover depicted the character "Brigham" from the series. While there were extensive alterations made to the figure itself, most of the work centered around making the background appear to "recede" properly, which is usually effected in painting by color temperature (cool recedes, warm advances) and contrast, which is why the final version has a slight "halo" around the foreground figure and landscape, an effect which I had noticed in art but also in photography.

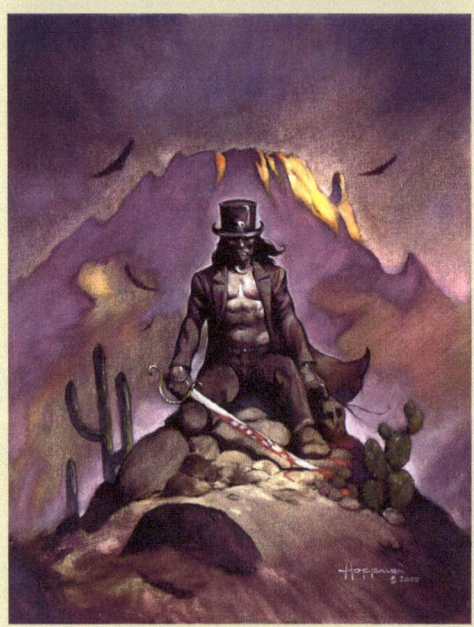
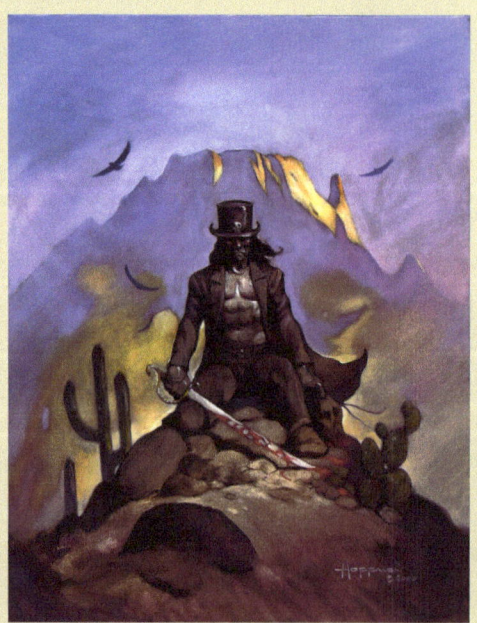
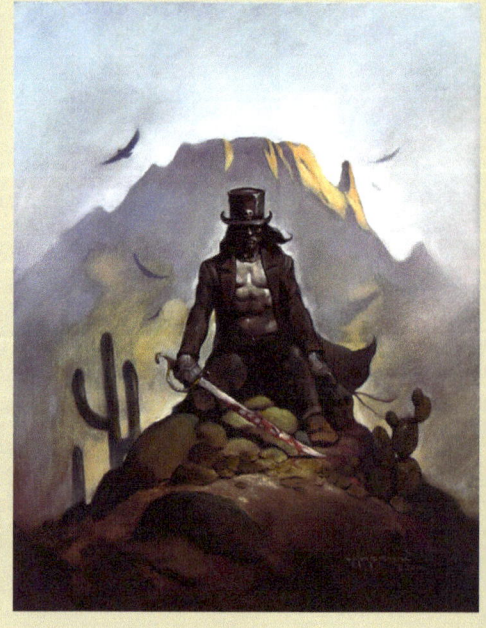

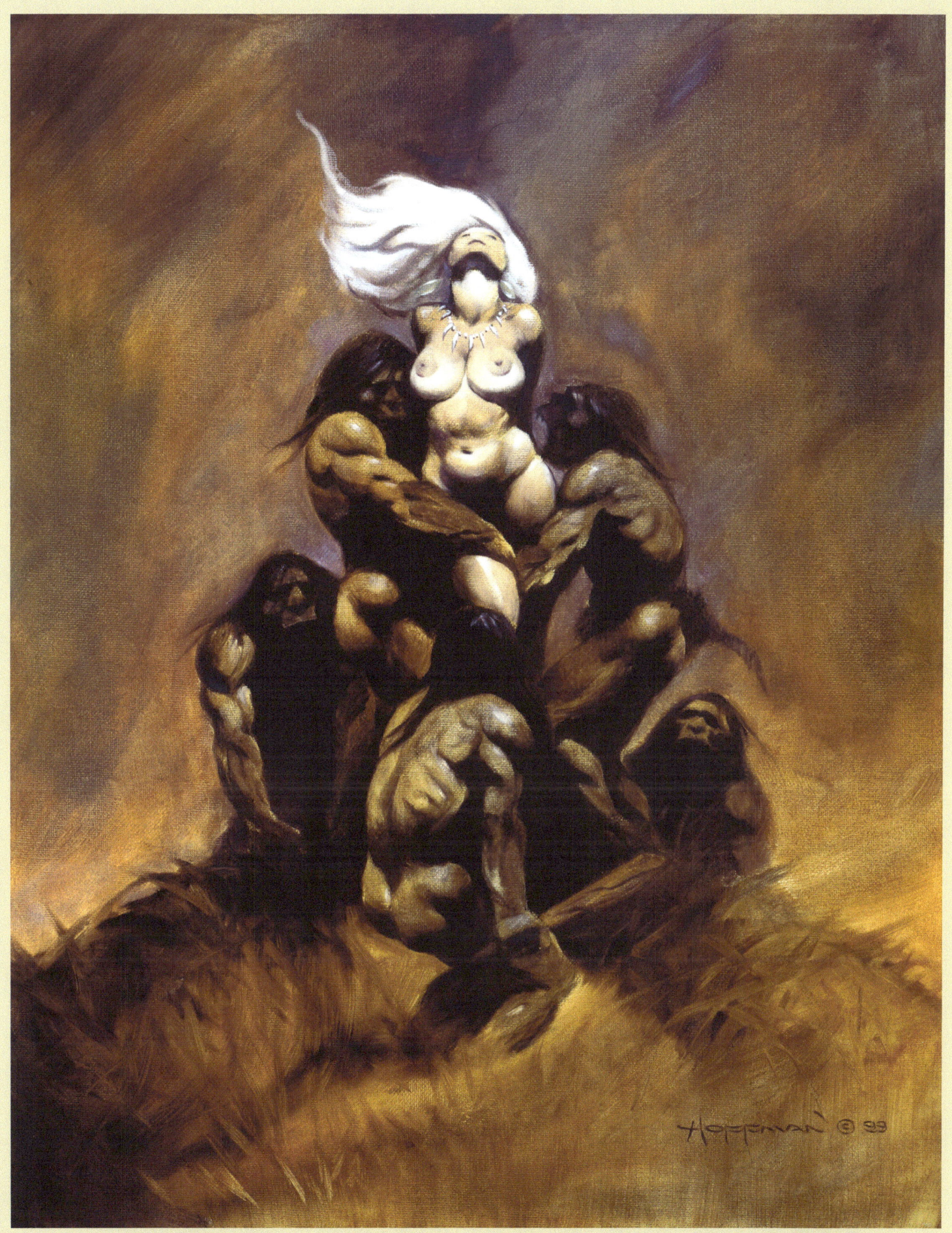

An oil painting from 1999 titled "Captive", which seemed to push all the right buttons for the fans at that time.

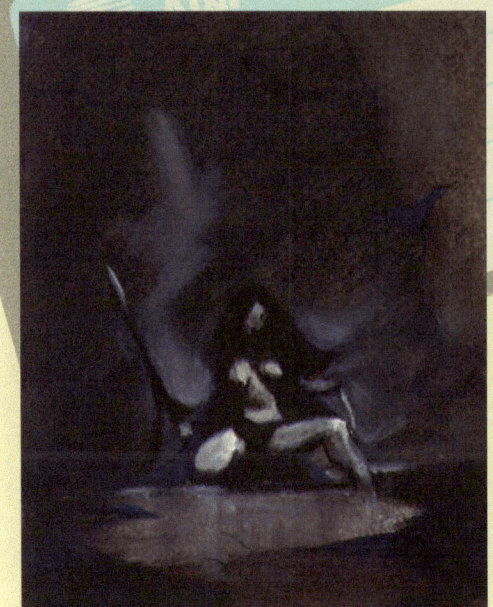

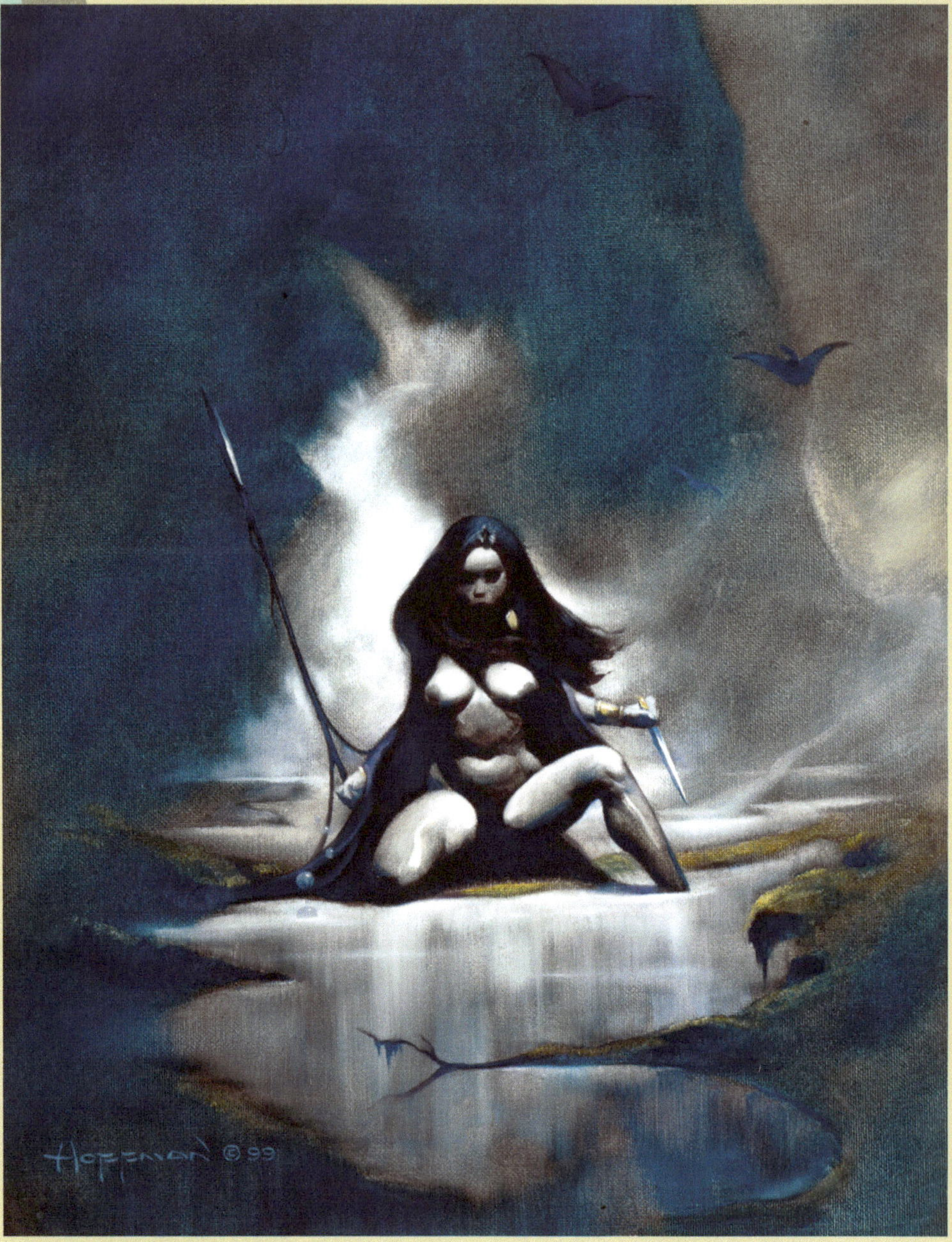

Almost all my early paintings had preliminary rough sketches or color studies, only years later did I abandon the method and begin working straight onto the canvas from my head.

Above is the blue-green, watery *Huntress* with its small 3"x4" oil study.

Below left is *Neanderthal Visitation,* which I consider a highly inspired idea for the time, that is alien involvement in human affairs during some lost prehistoric era. The painting was sold to a friend but later "lost" in a house fire; is should have still been in an undamaged area, but it is more likely that a rogue Firemen appropriated it.

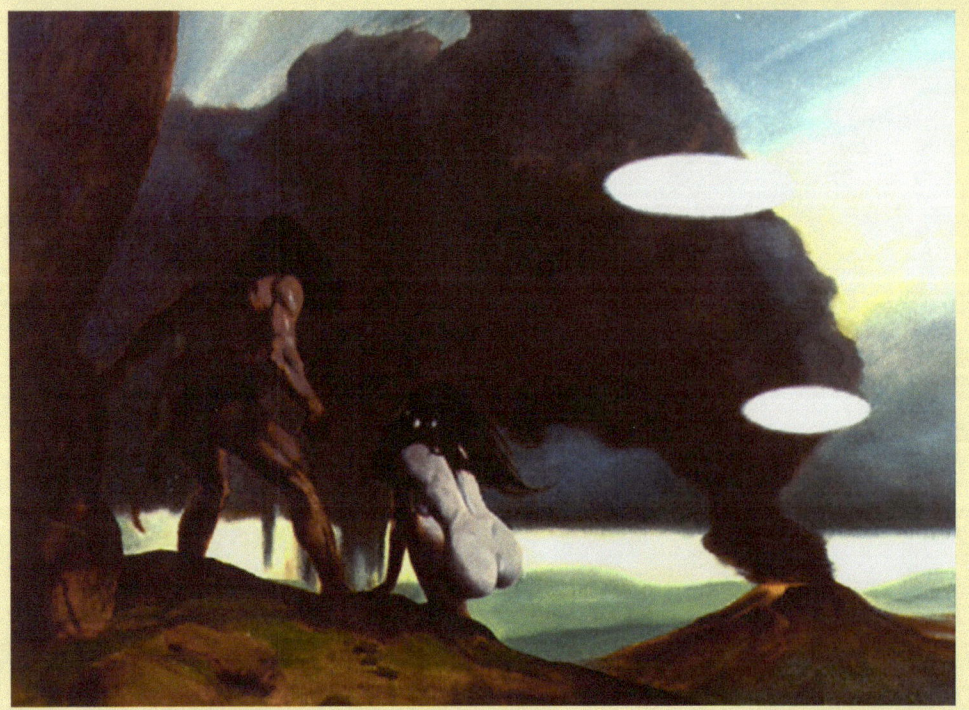

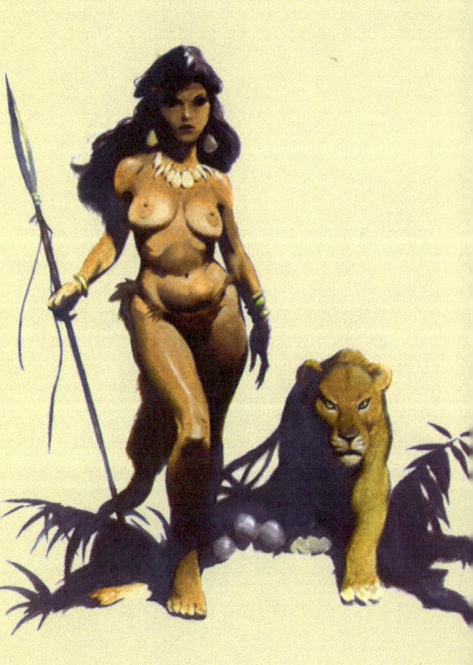

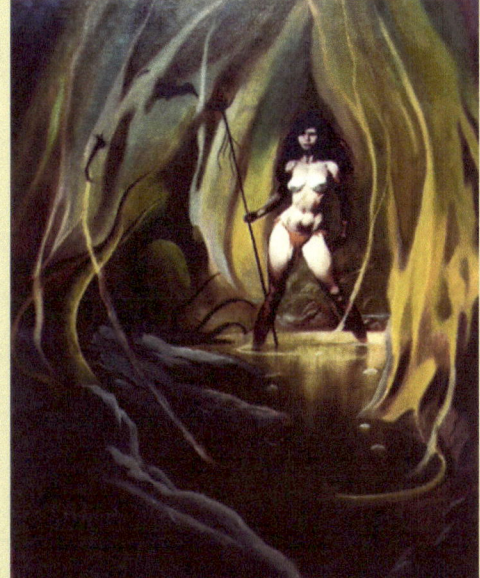

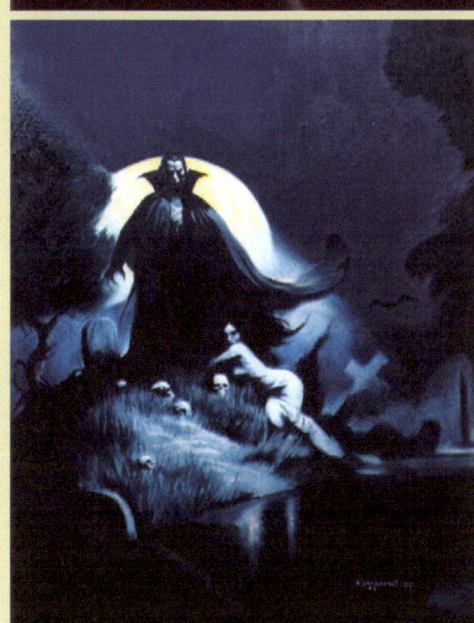

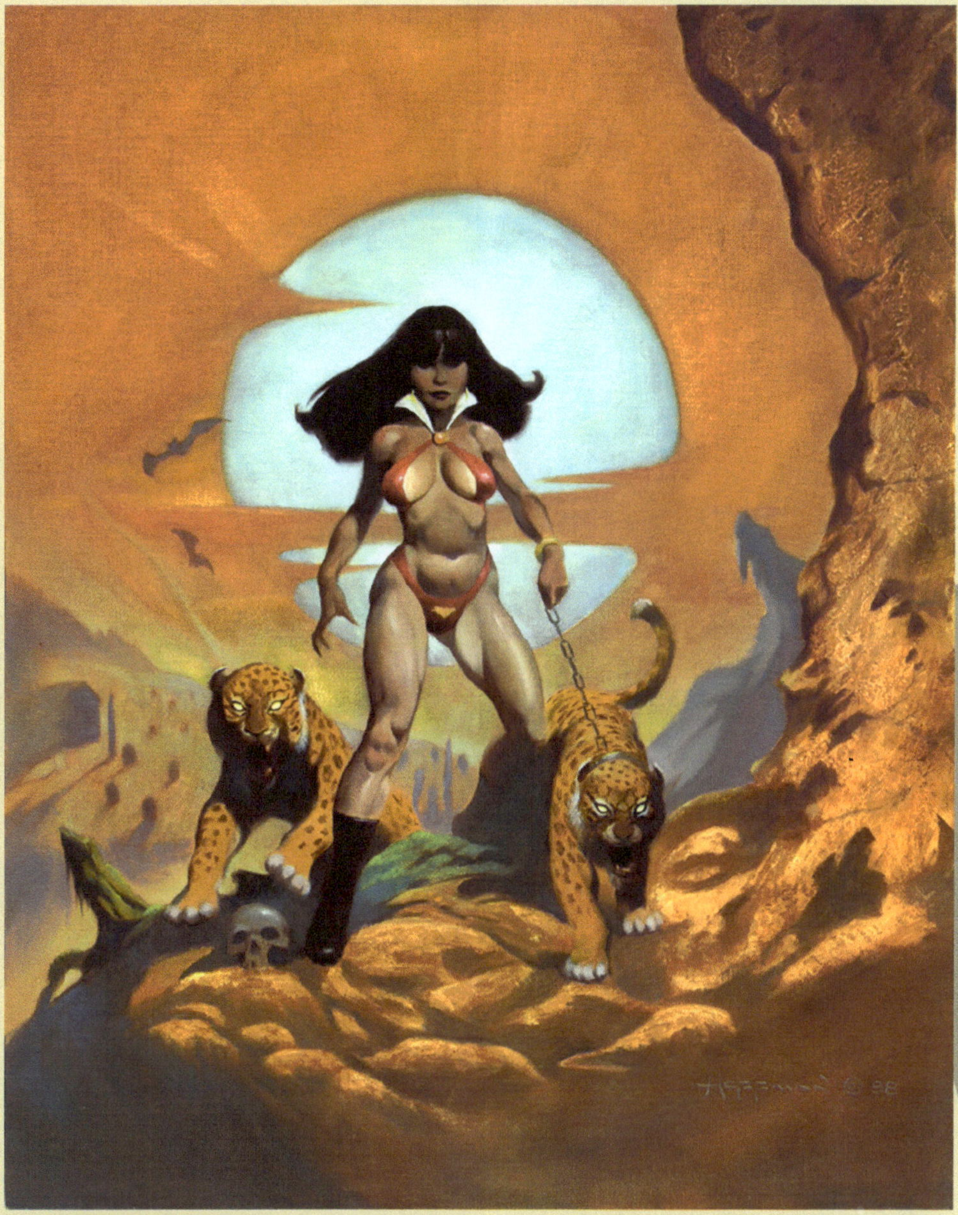

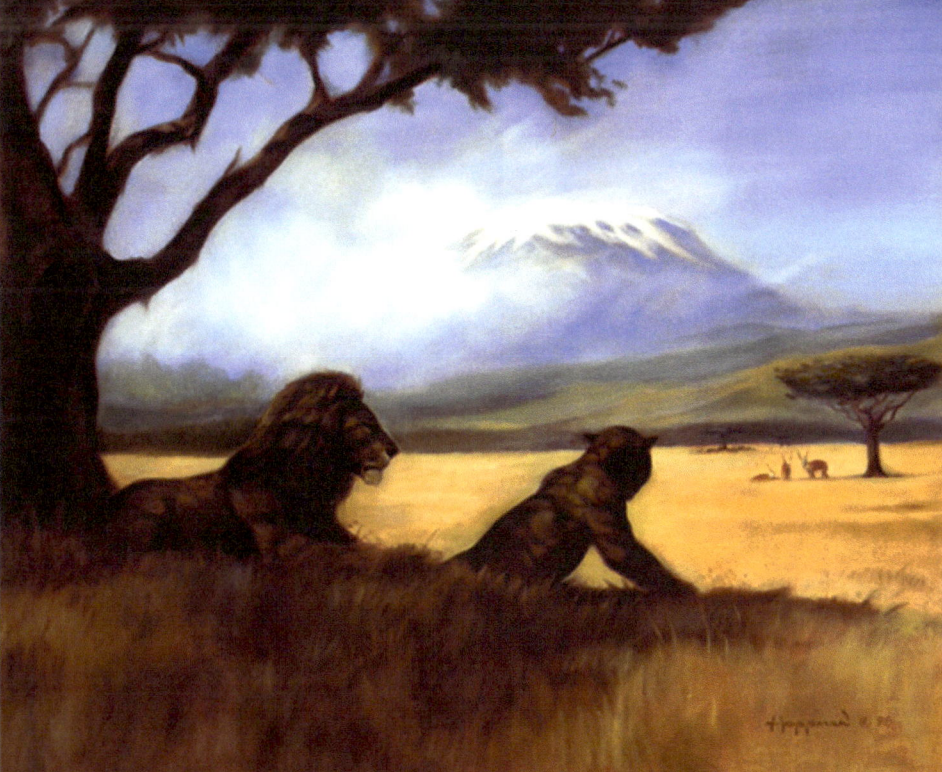

On this page are several oil paintings I did as far back as 1996. At top left is *Green Pool,* the first "Fantasy"-oriented painting I ever did. Below it is *Dracula*, which used "Prussian Blue" oil paint; *Kilamanjaro* is at bottom left, at right *Drakulon* and its rough.

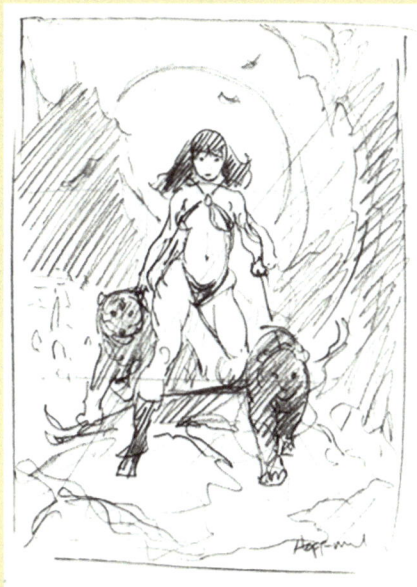

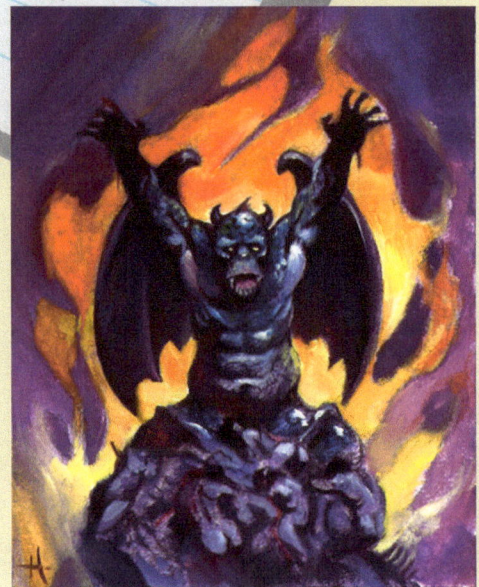

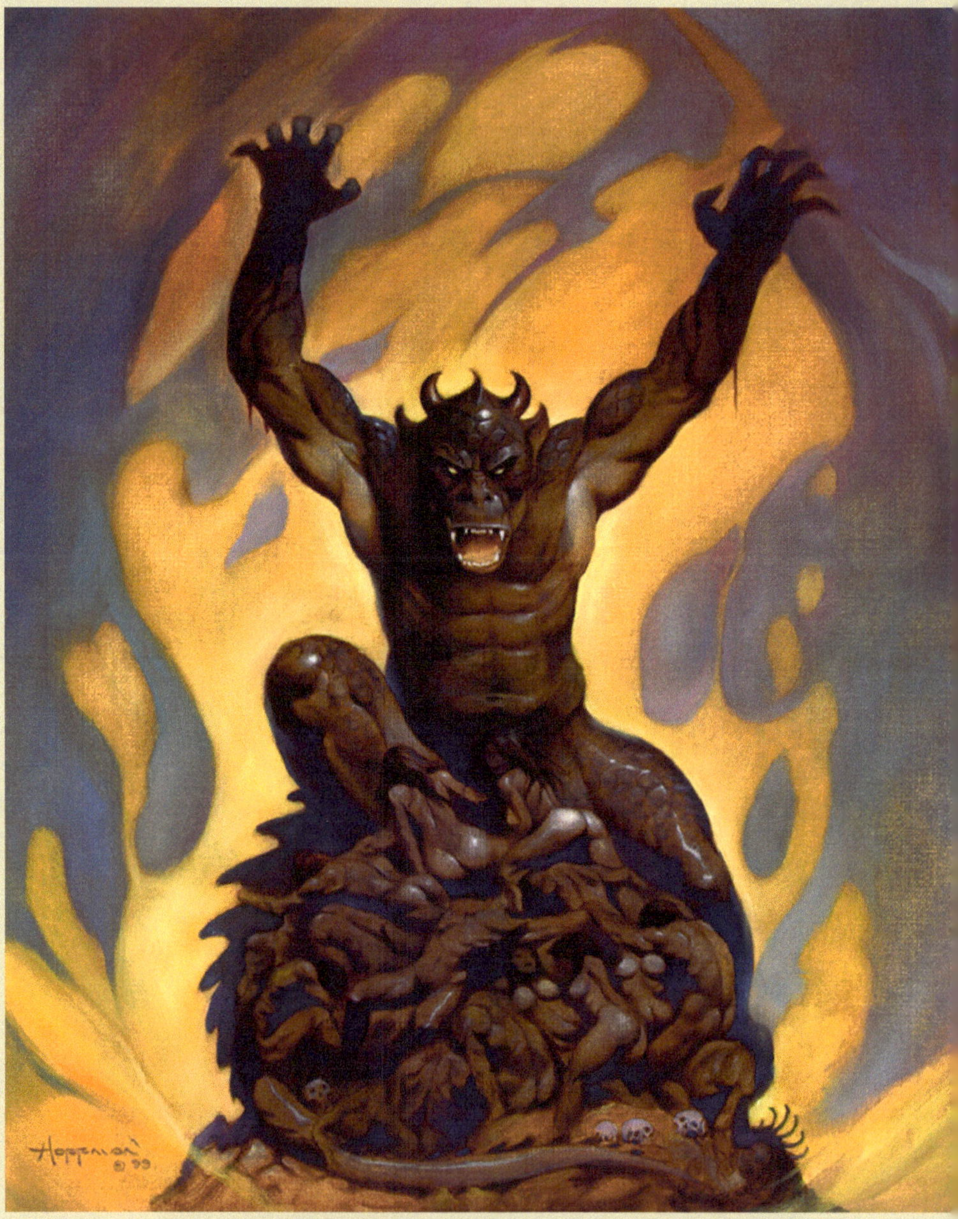

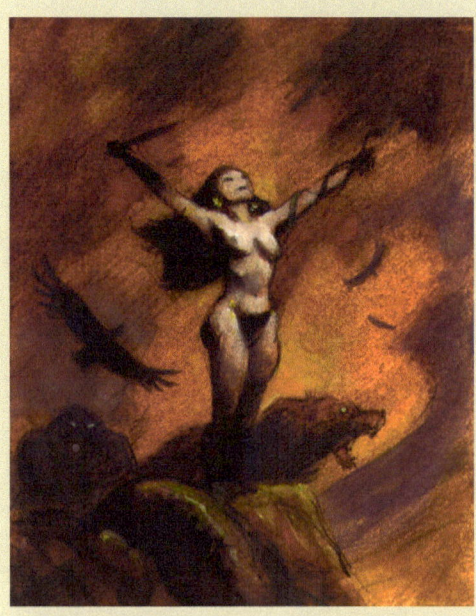

Another rough at top left for a final painting called *King Demon*, commissioned as a cover image for a "Death Metal" magazine (pictured at bottom left). At center left is a rough for the painting appearing on page one of this book; below are two more oils, the *Indian Girl* which appeared in *Sorceress II*, and *Highland Girl*, a private commission.

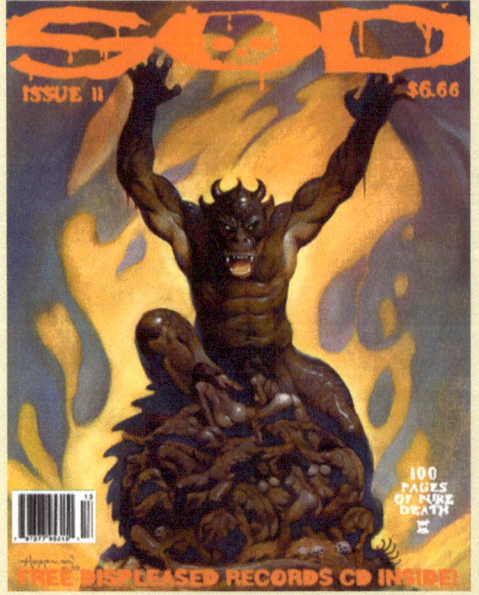

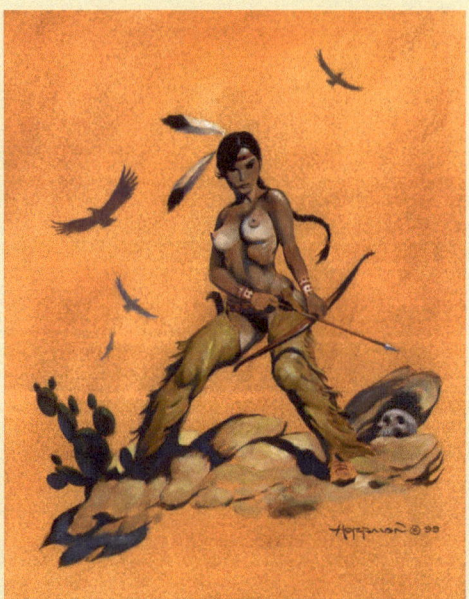

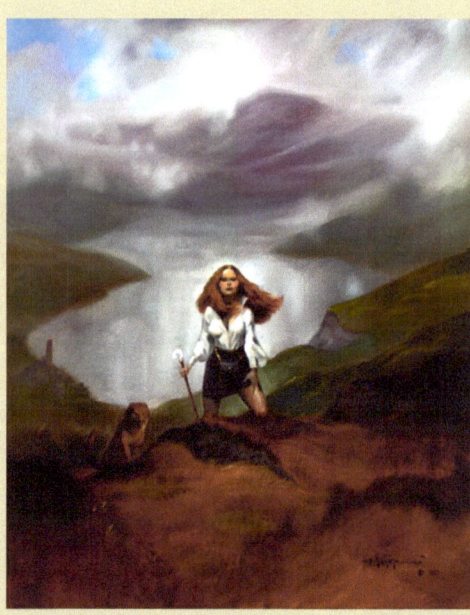

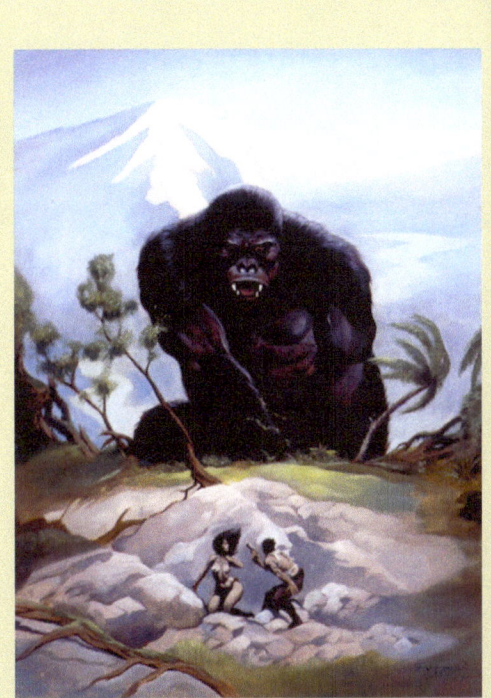

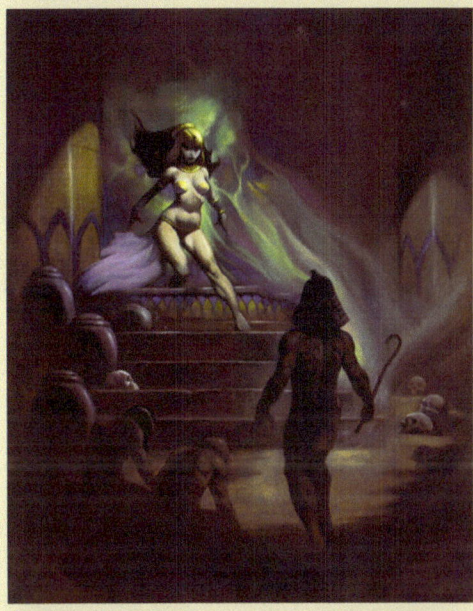

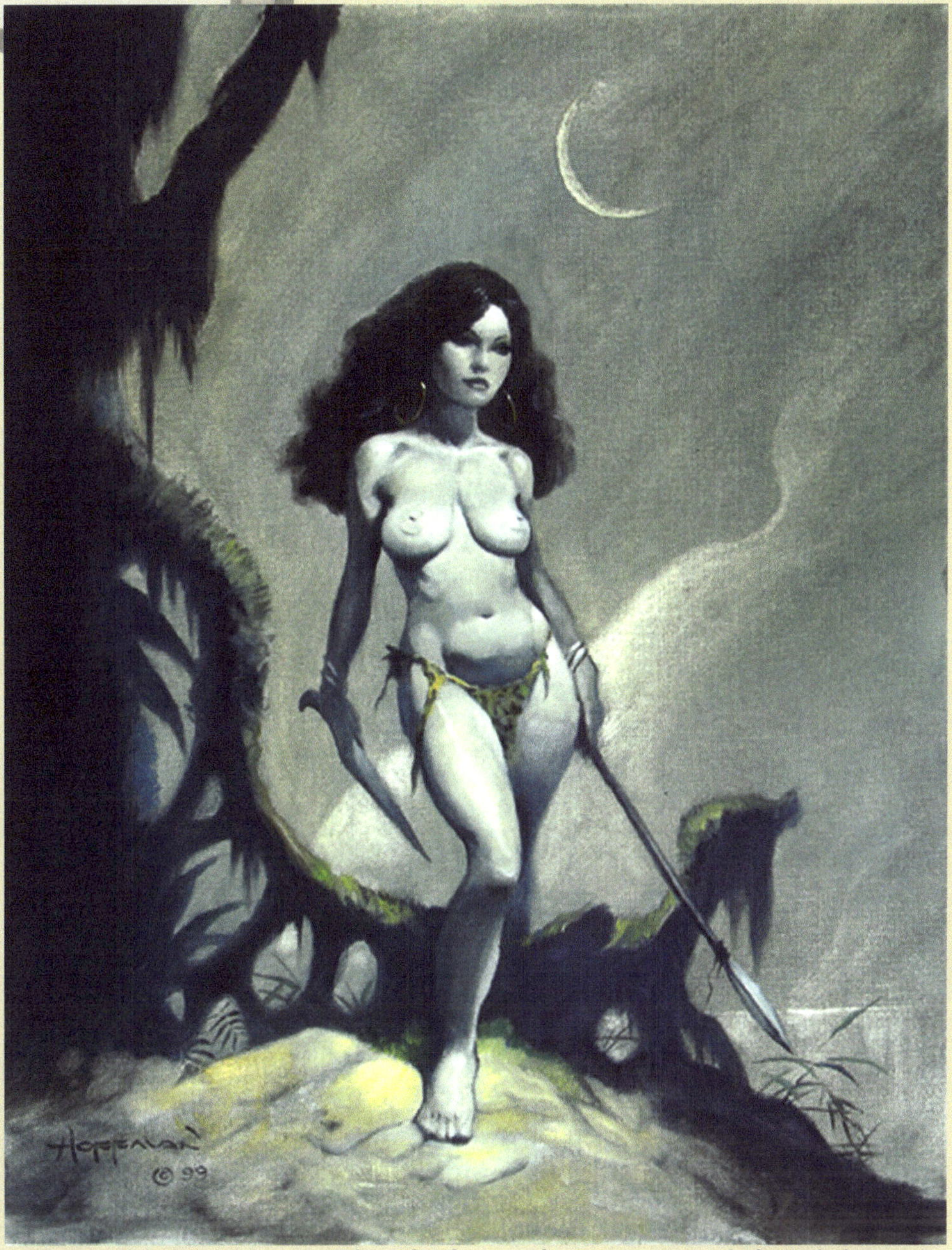

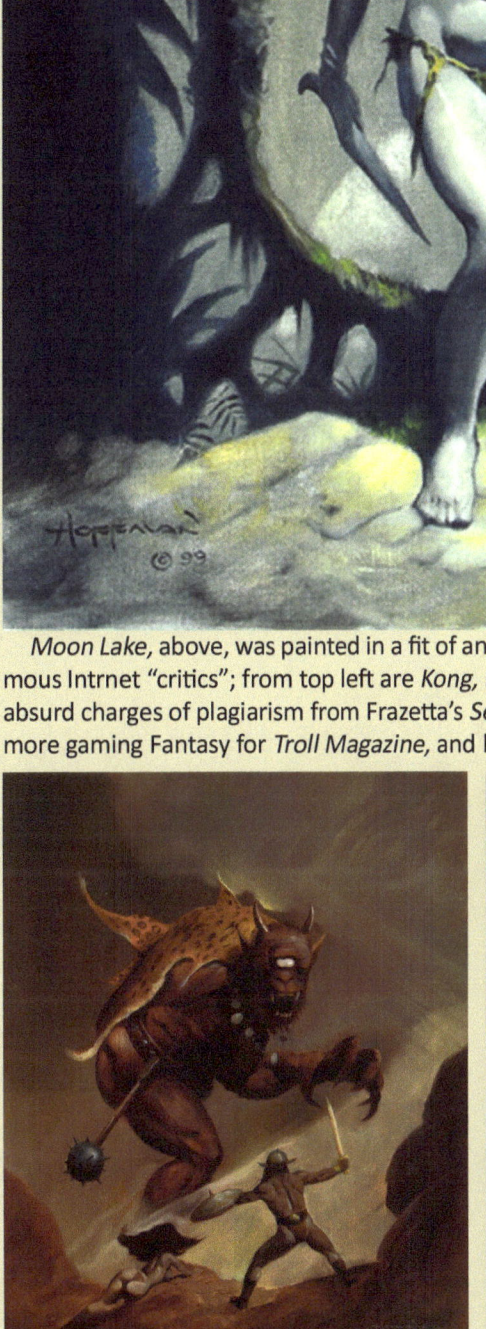

Moon Lake, above, was painted in a fit of anger after a severe round of attacks by anonymous Intrnet "critics"; from top left are *Kong, Egyptian Princess, Sea Goddess*--which drew absurd charges of plagiarism from Frazetta's *Sea Witch* from a certain art "atelier"; *Fachan,* more gaming Fantasy for *Troll Magazine,* and lastly *Boudicca,* a legendary warrior woman.

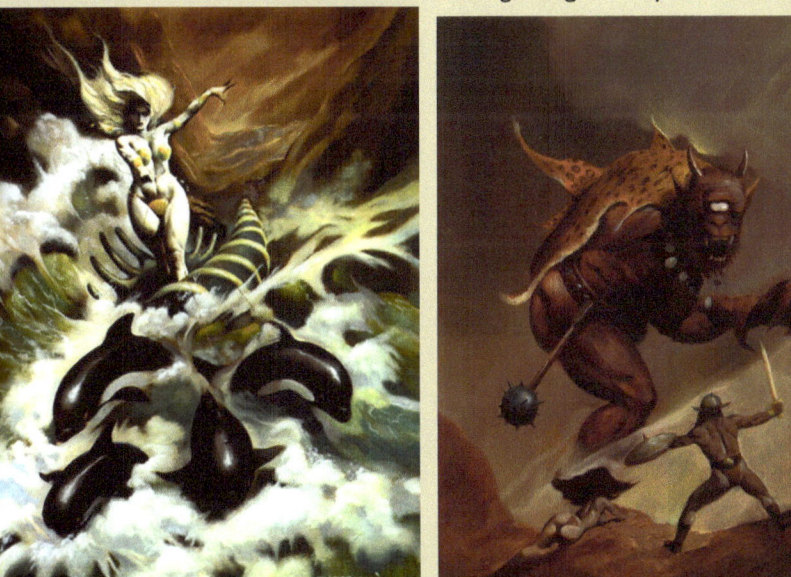

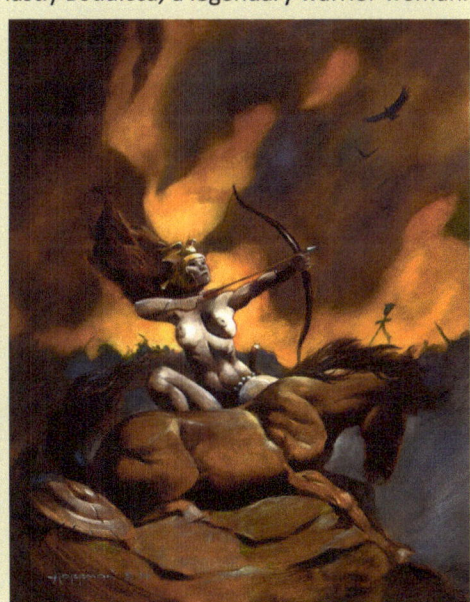

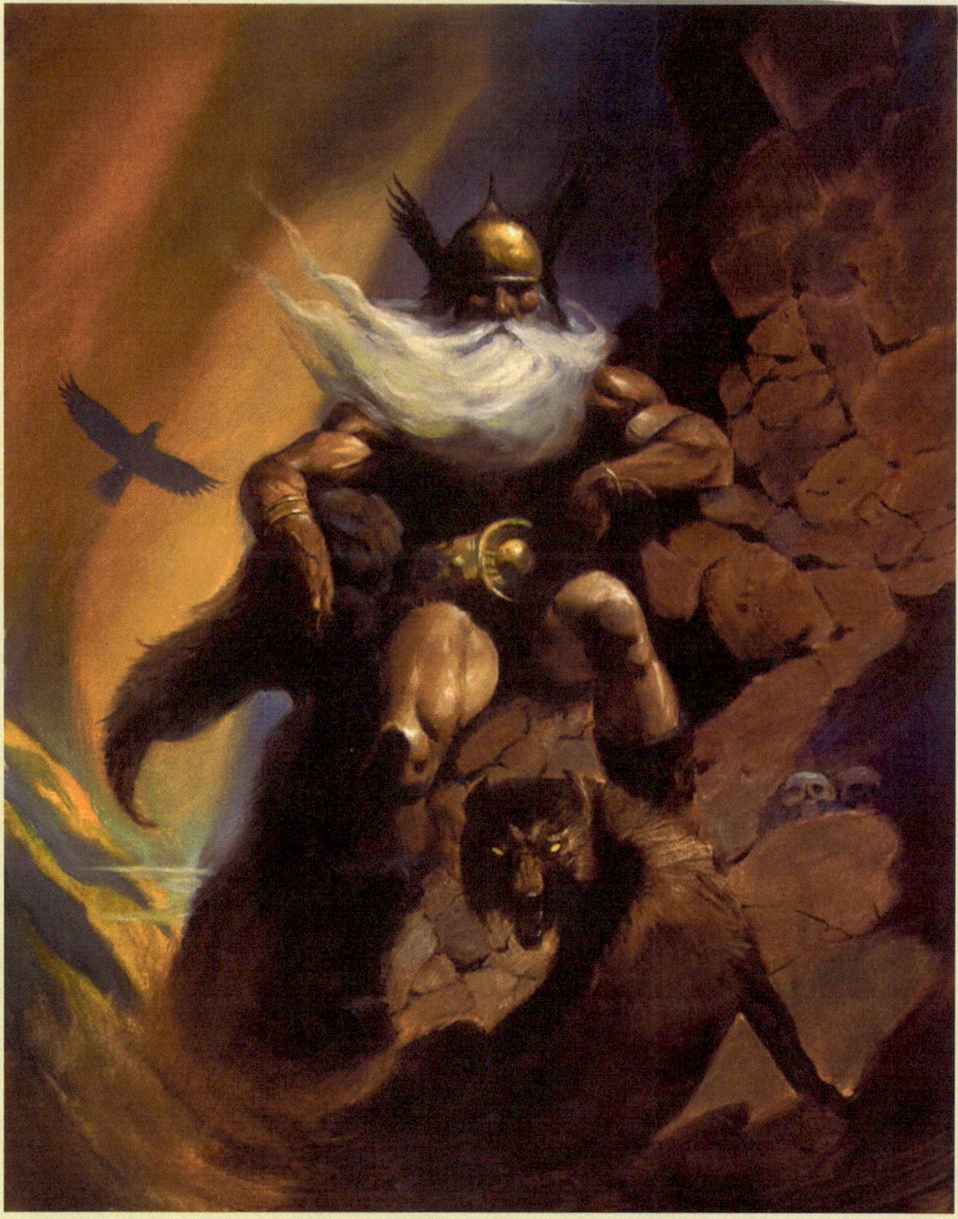

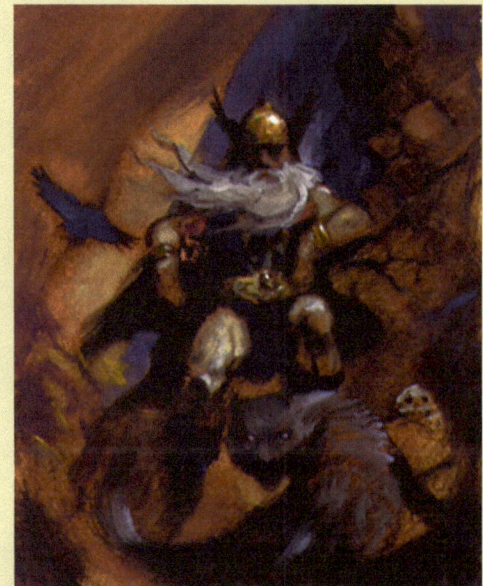

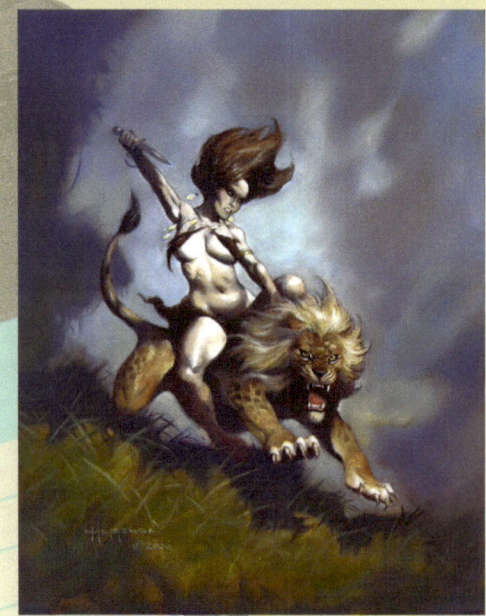

Above is *Odin* and its small oil rough, depicting the Norse god with his wolf and crow companions; below right, another paternal figure, *Poseidon,* created for a scuba company (compare to later version, next page); below, a private commission for a dragon-lover; at left an obscure mythologic character for a defunct Gaming company *Troll Magazine.*

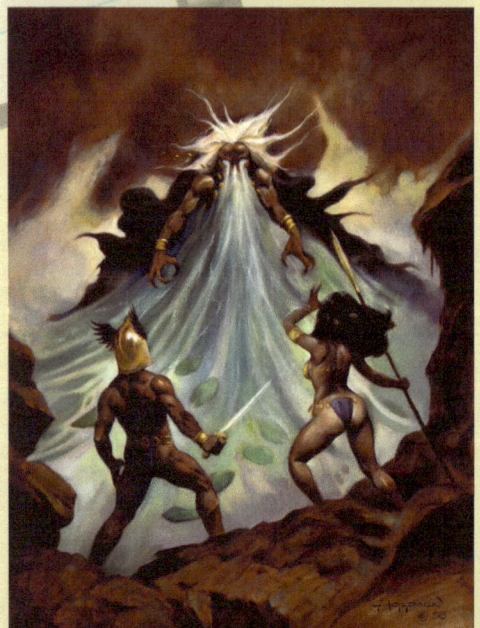

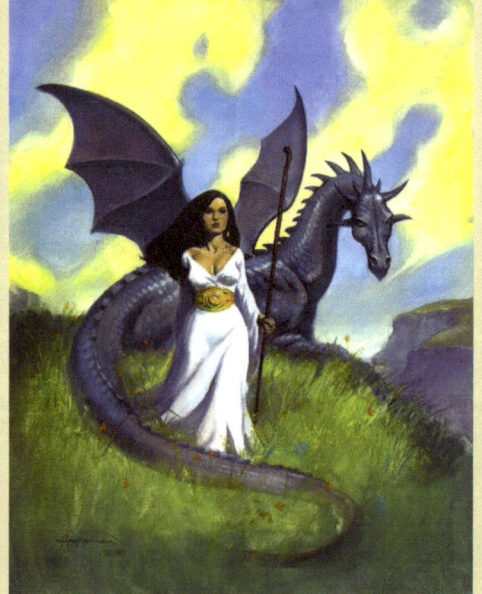

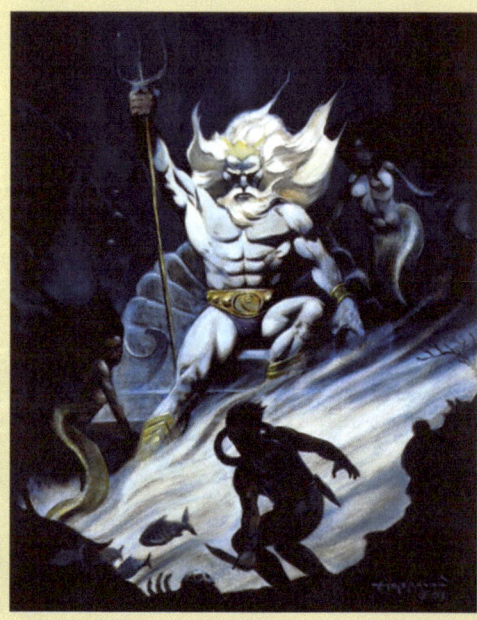

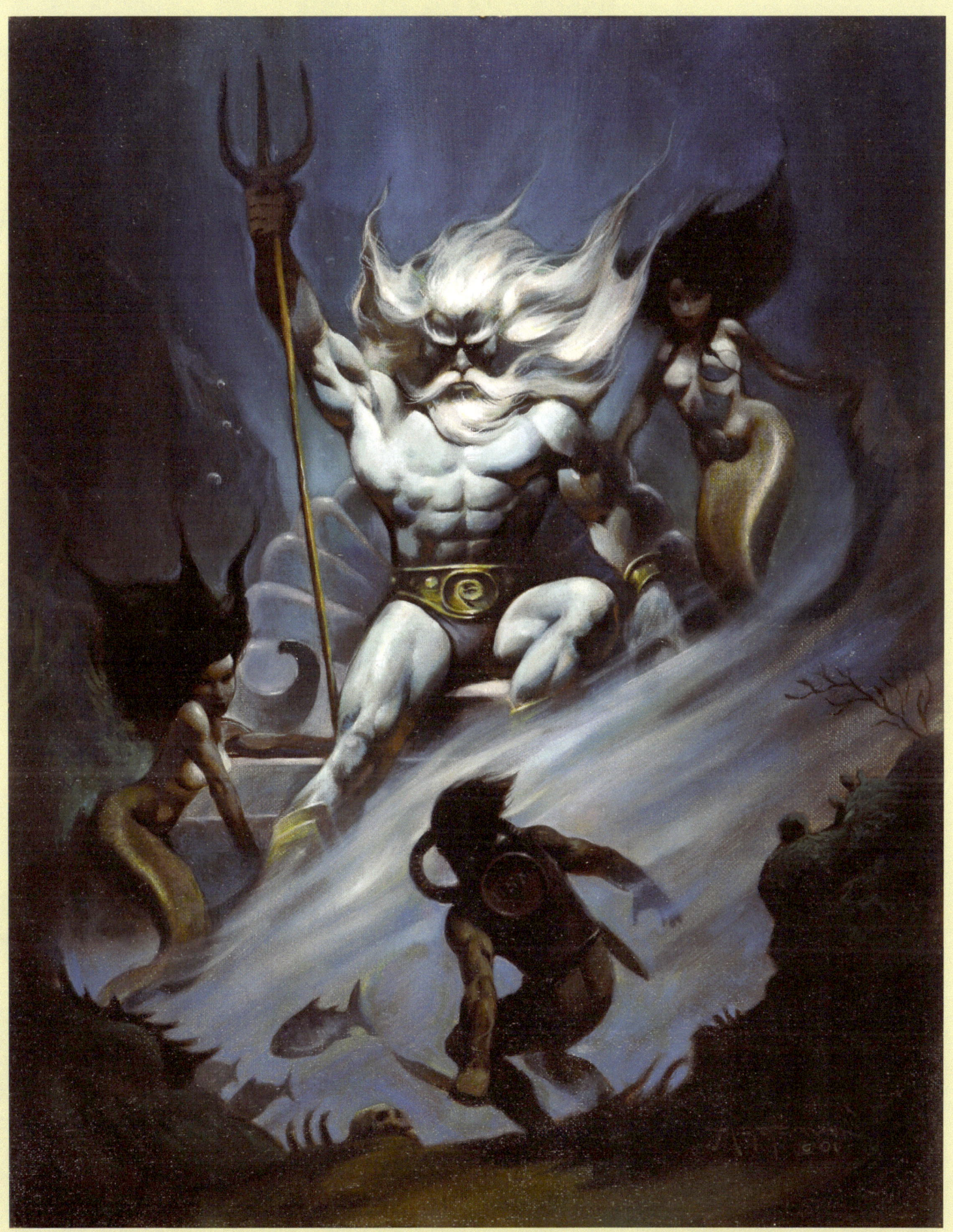

A polished, retouched version of "Poseidon", my first painting photographed digitally upon arriving in Albuquerque, NM in 2001.

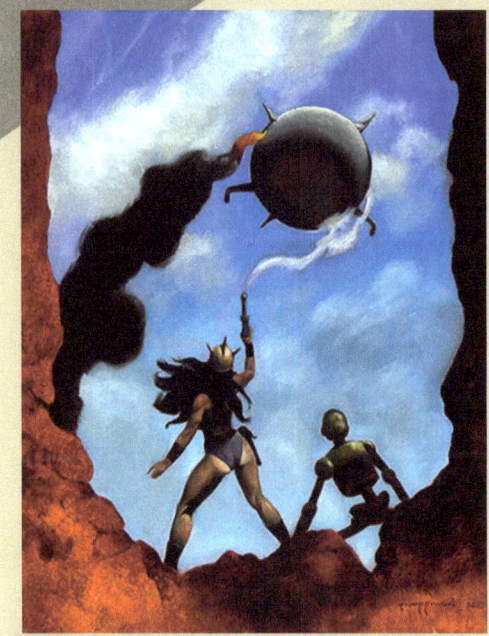

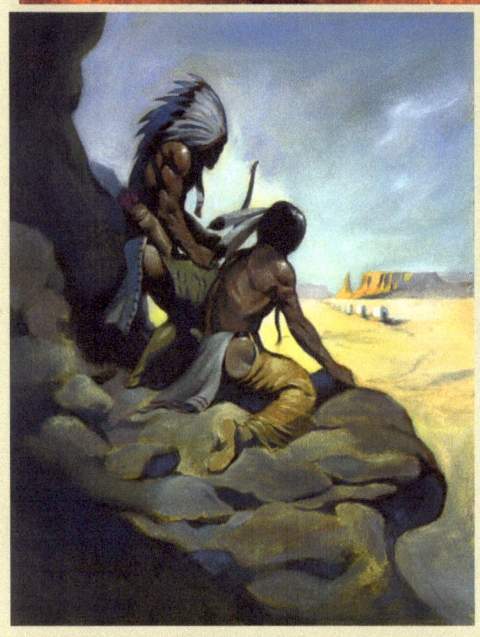

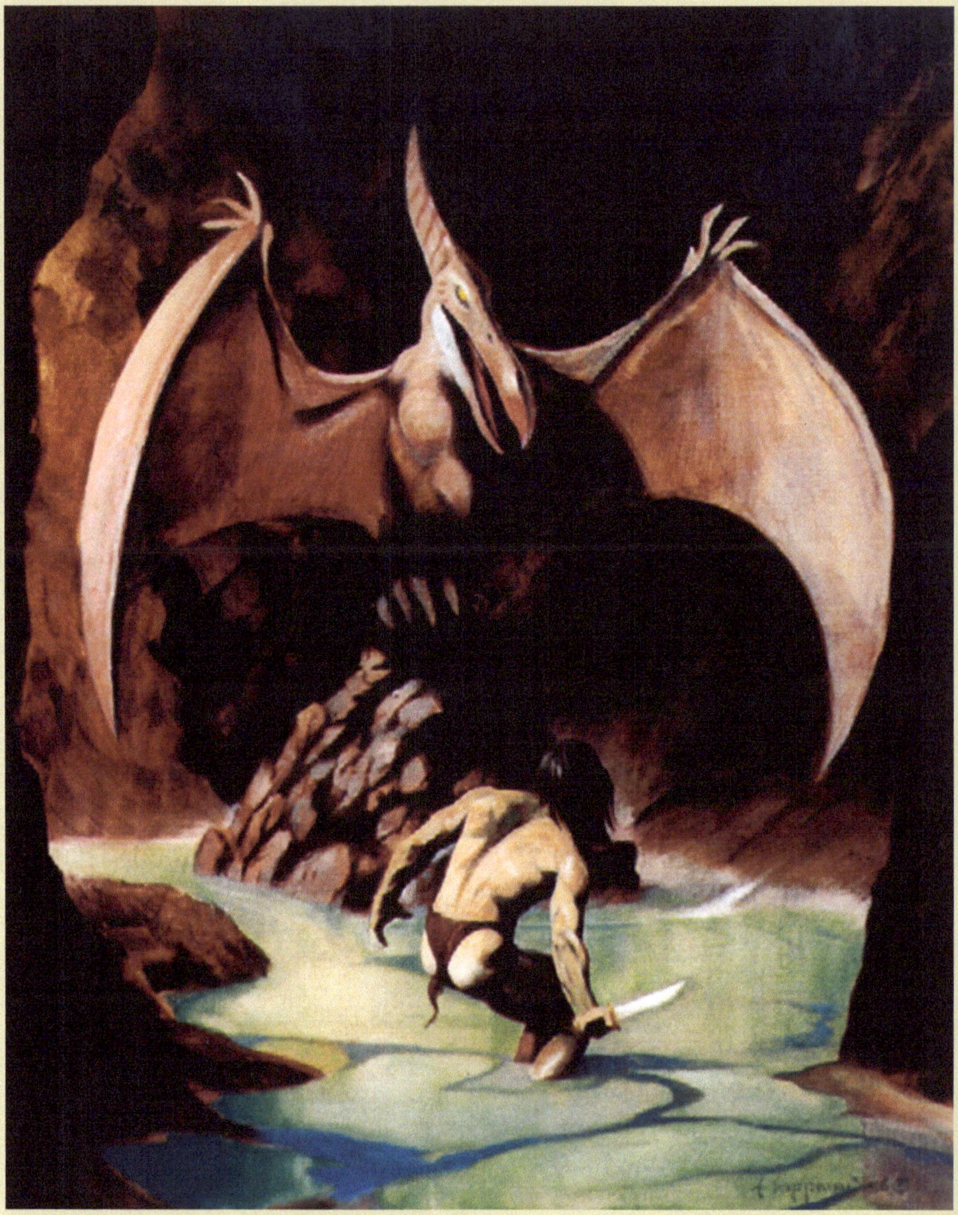

The top two images inspired me to paint new versions; *Steel Planet* (left) became *Slave Planet* (next page) and I recreated *Pterodactyl*, though I substituted a female figure in the later version. At bottom is *Egyptian Priestess*, which was a stab at a cover to *Sorceress II* but wound up on the back cover instead; center is *Panther Girl*, and last, *Cyclops*.

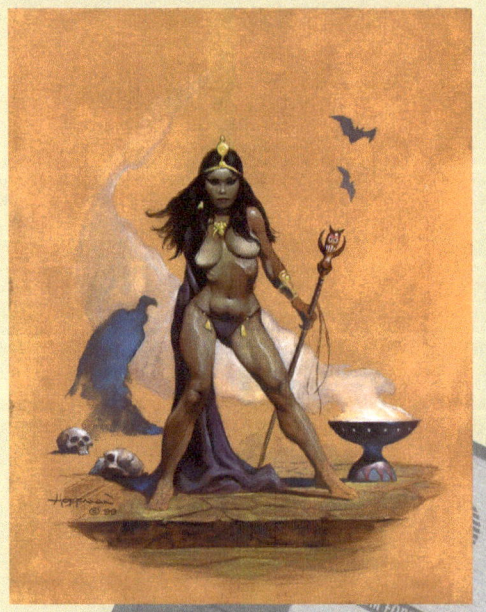

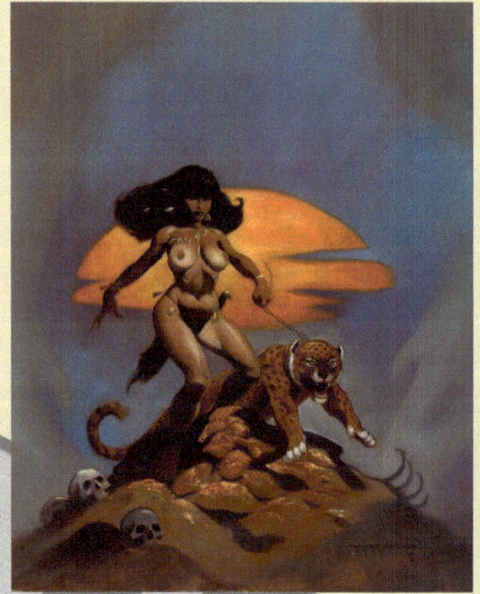

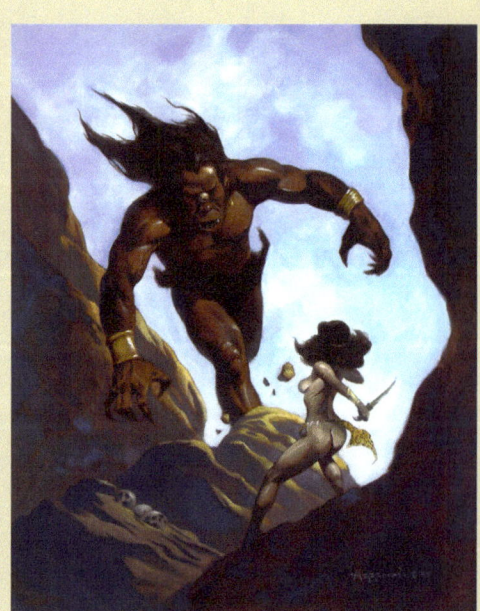

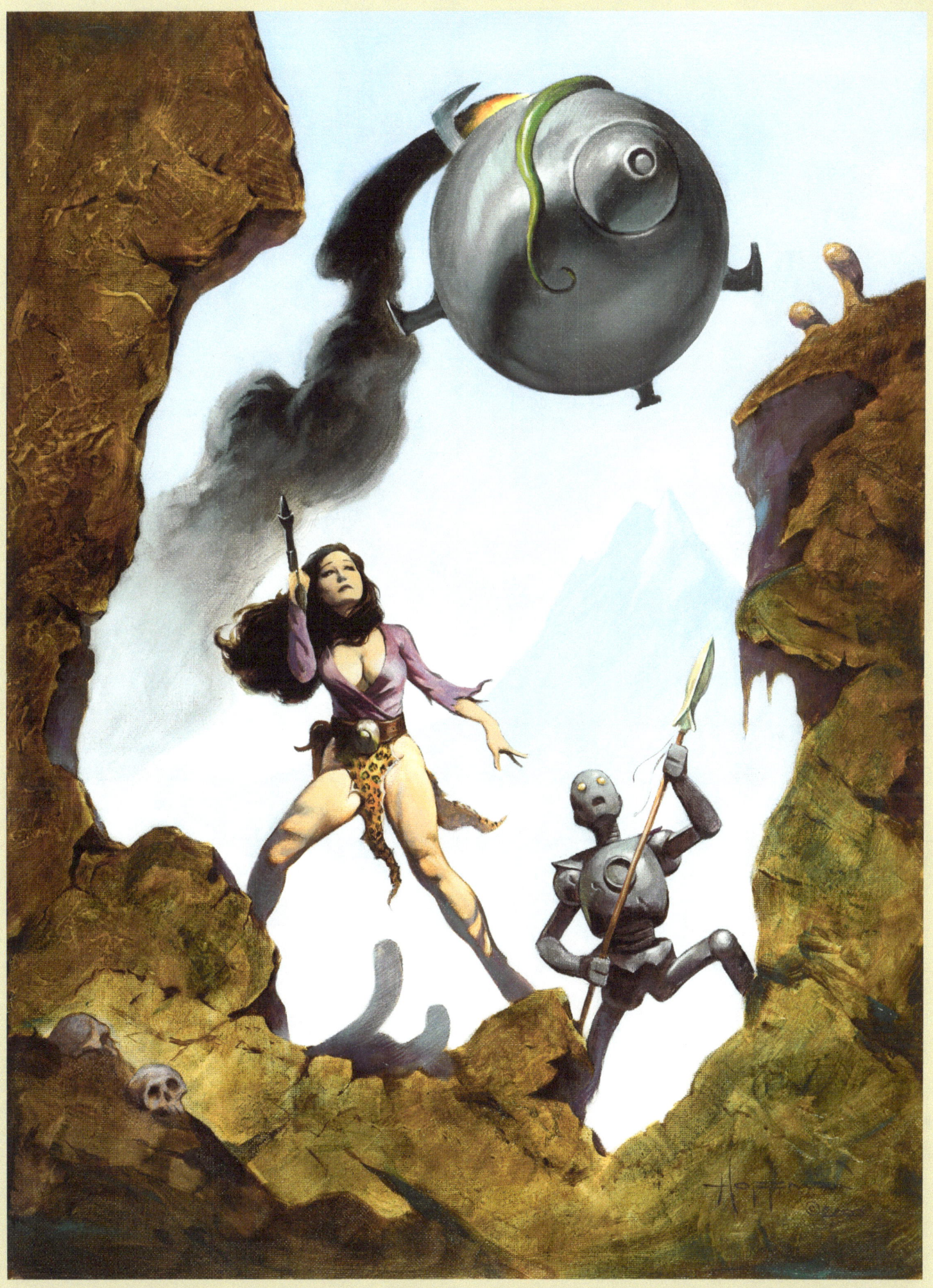

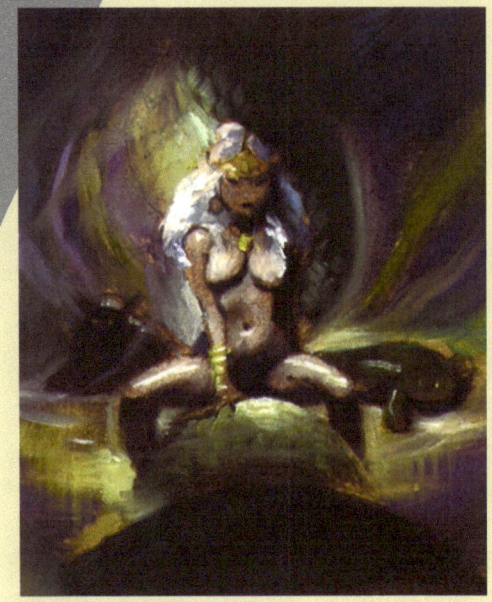

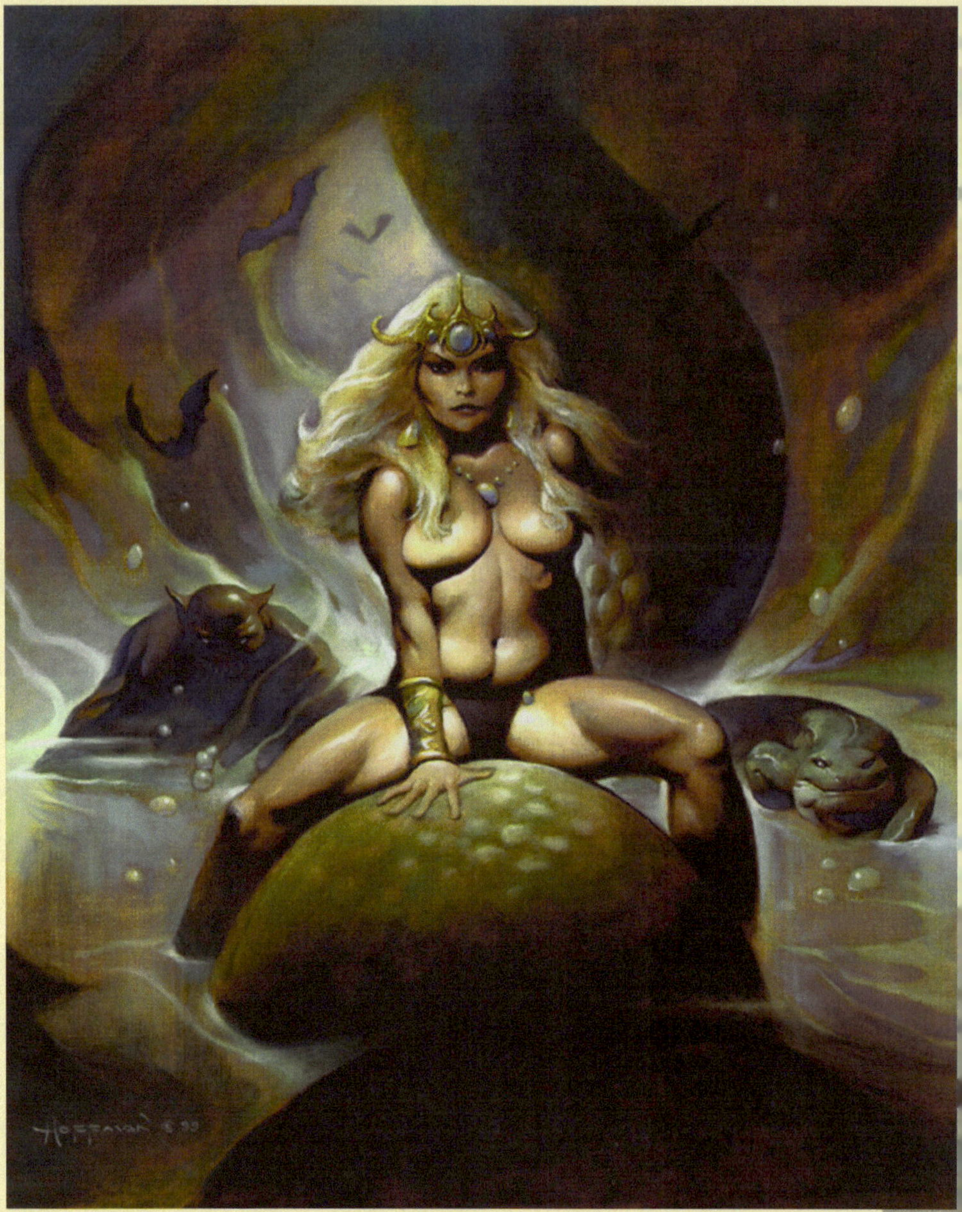

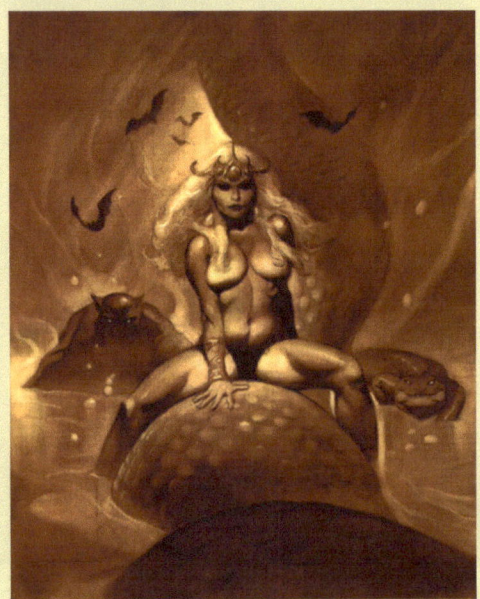

The cover for *Sorceress II* was considered important around the studio--or corner of the living room--and I did many roughs and mockups, like the preliminary design at top left, ultimately developed in to the final cover. Other designs, below center and right, were unused; the *Sorceress* logo is not a font but rather a hand-drawn element.

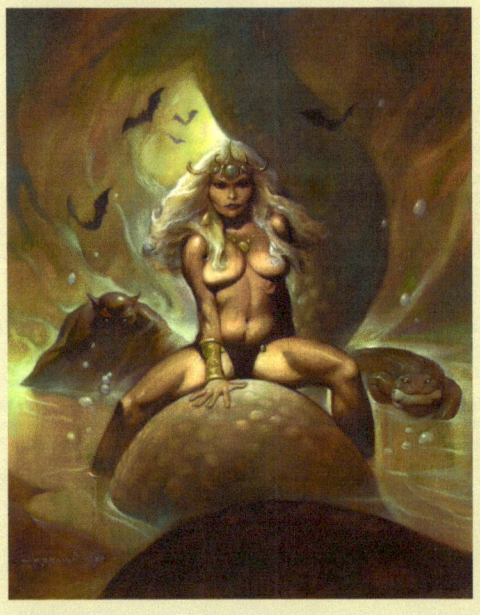

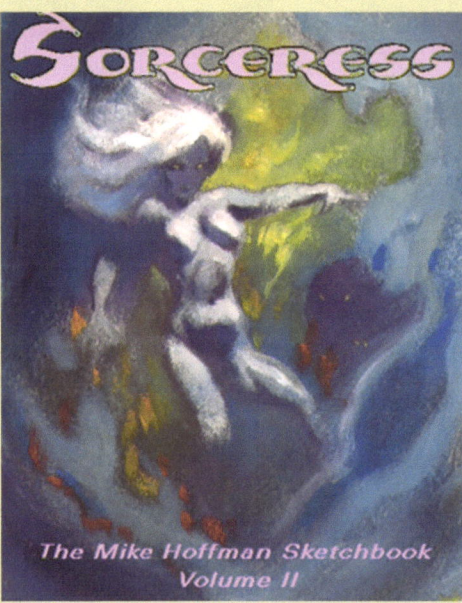

The Mike Hoffman Sketchbook
Volume II

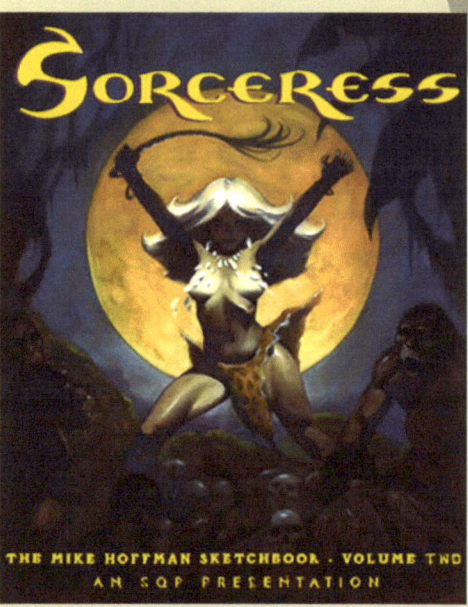

THE MIKE HOFFMAN SKETCHBOOK · VOLUME TWO
AN SQP PRESENTATION

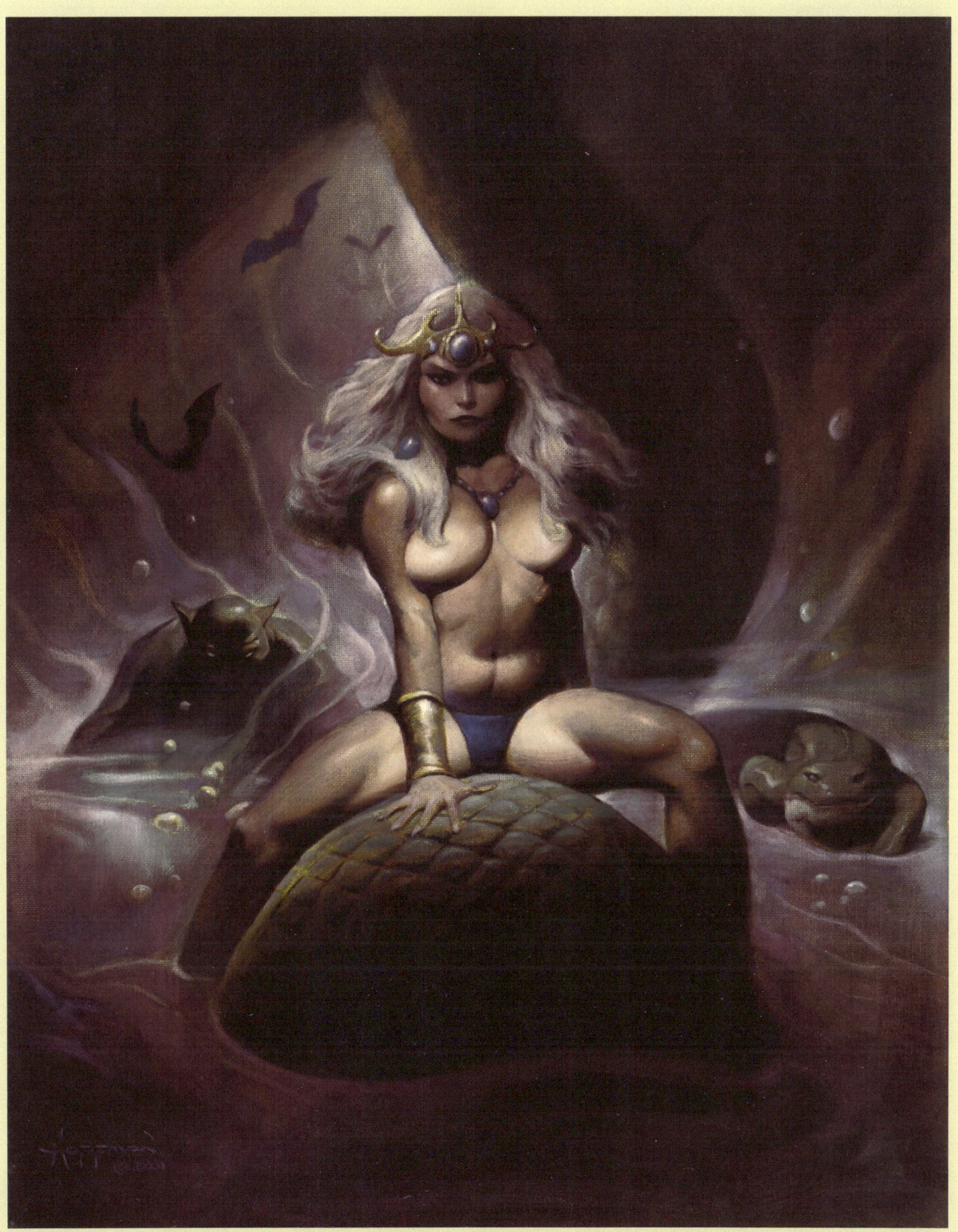

Not knowing yet the formal rule that a painting should be either about light. color or value, I wrestled--by sheer force of will and un-trained eyesight--the piece "Sorceress II" away from color and towards light in a mad, final session at the close of 2000 (unpublished).

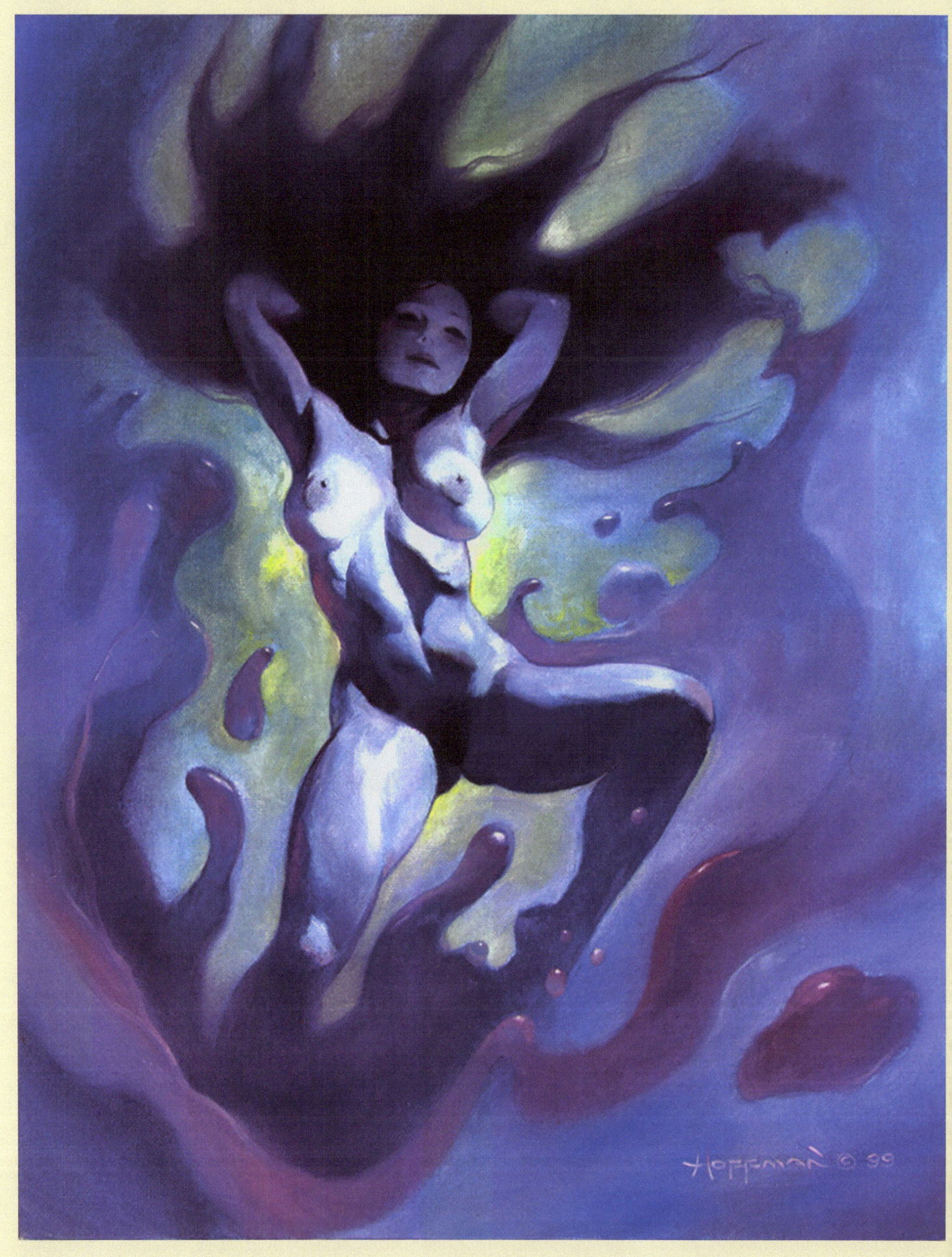

Created strictly for my own enjoyment, "Fantasy Girl" combined my fledgling painting skills with overt eroticism; oil on masonite.

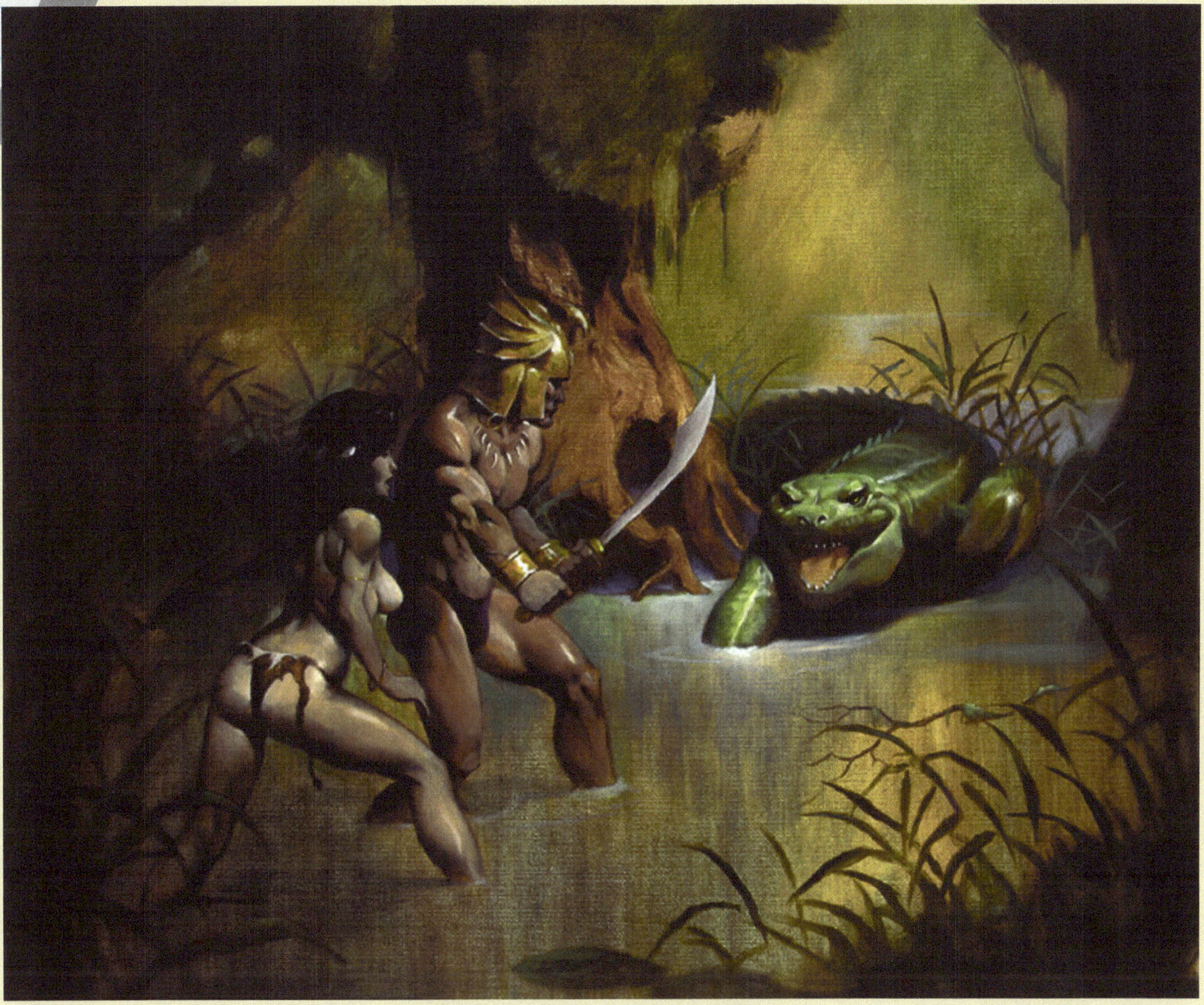

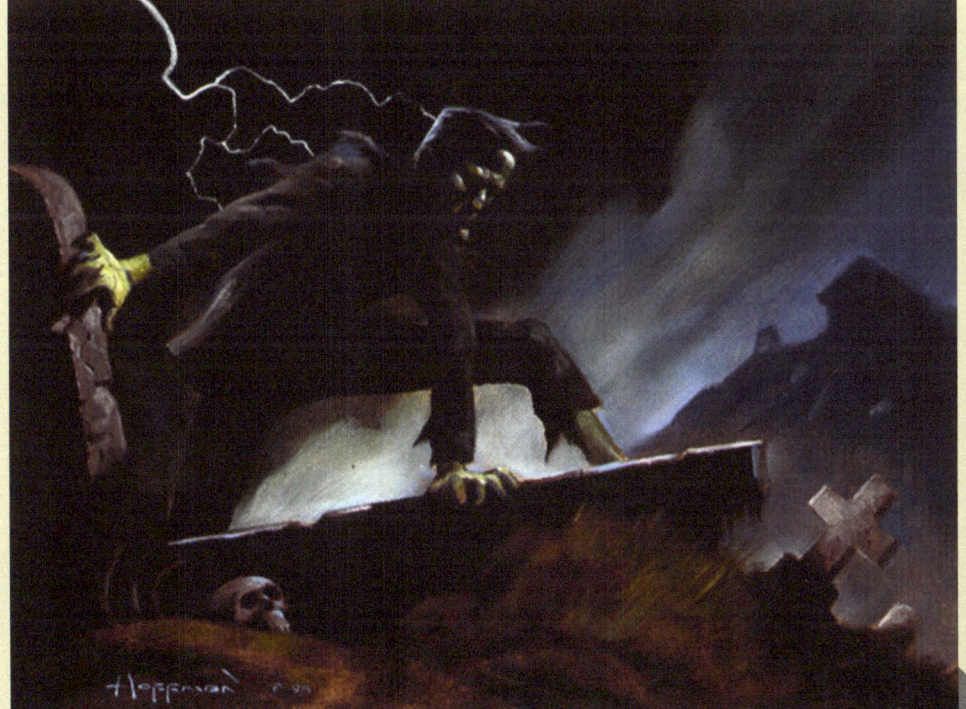

Above is *Saint George and the Dragon*, left, *Frankenstein*, below right *Sorceress*, the cover art for my first book circa 1999.

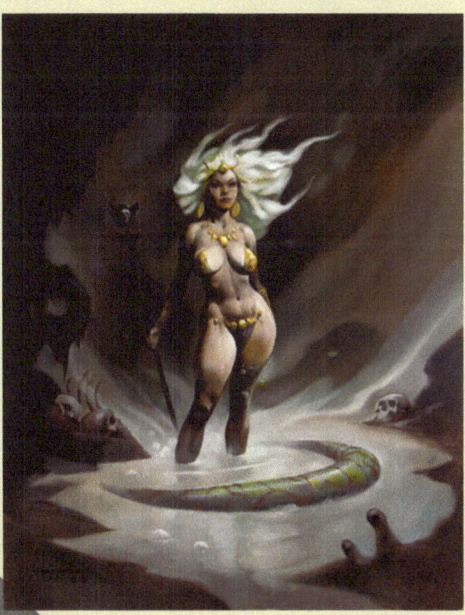

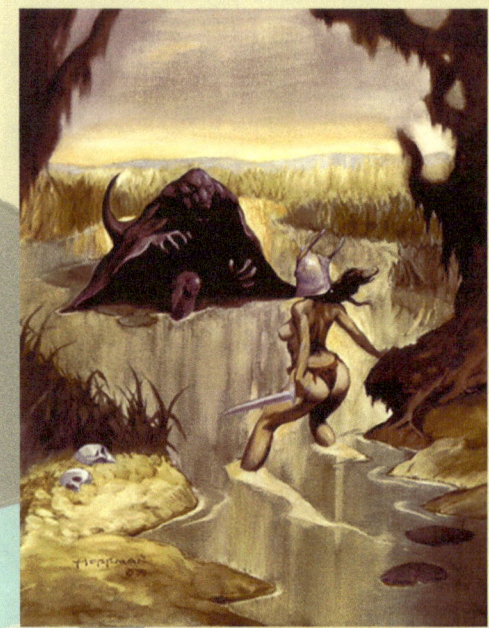

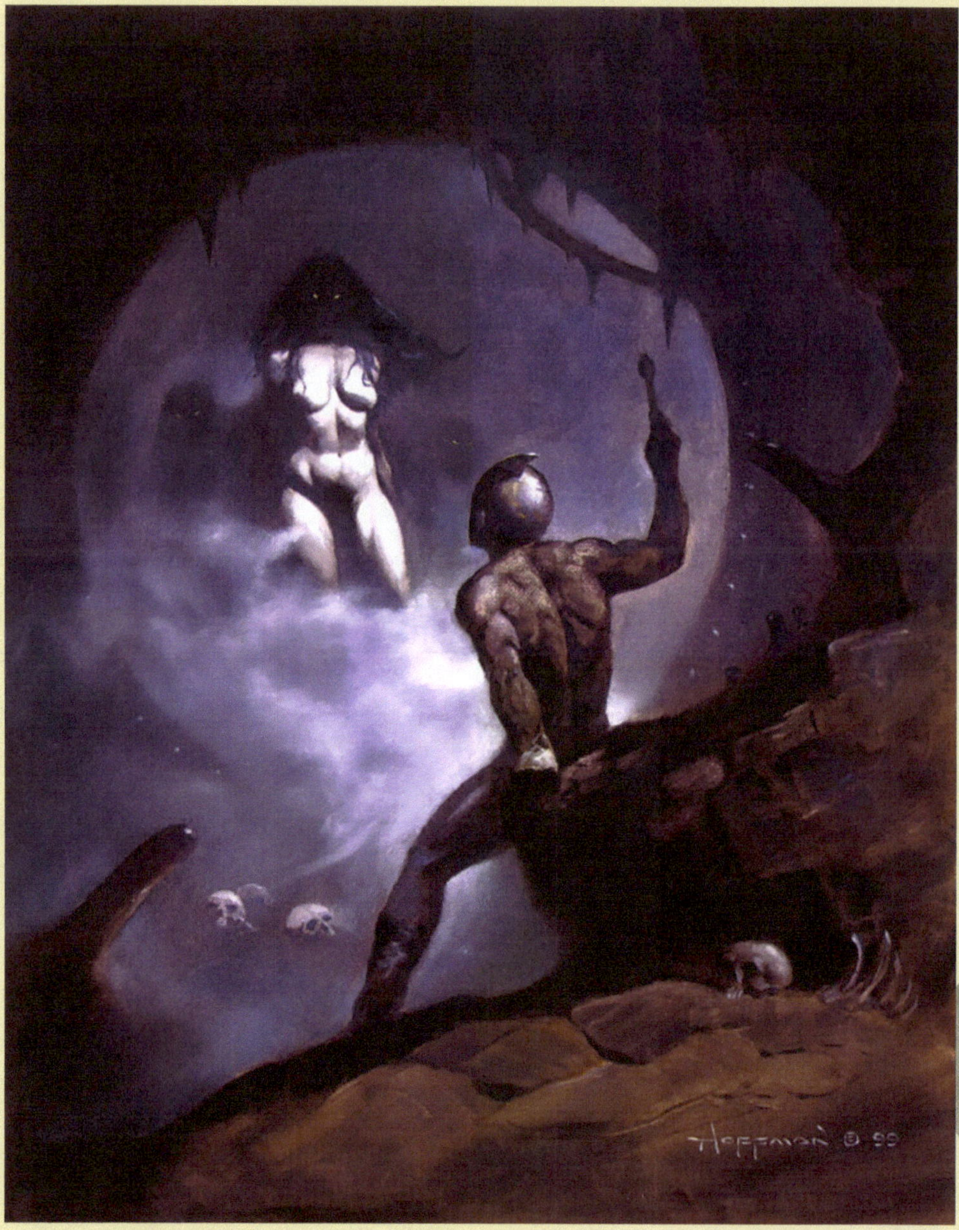

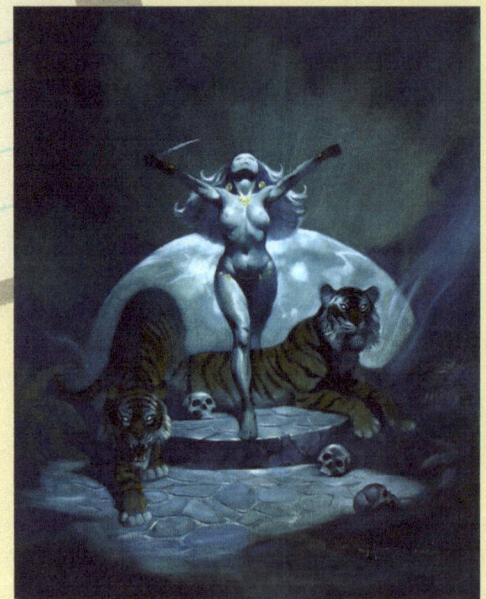

Later paintings seemed to get away from the simple geometries that made the early works effective, like the circles and triangles in *Star Women,* above. Top left: *Swamp Monster,* painted for an early convention appearance; below: Jungle and Western scenes.

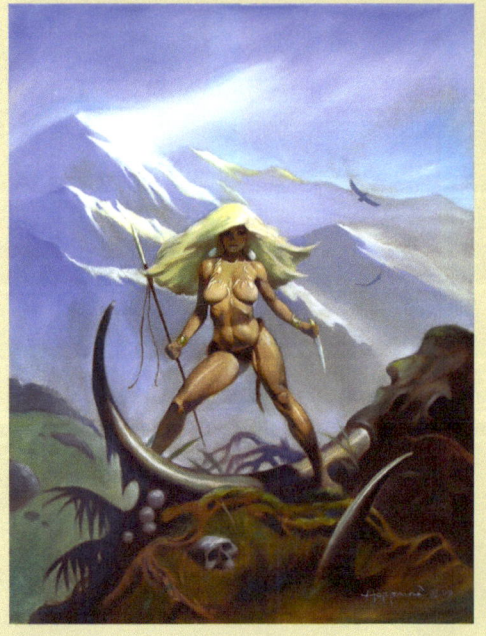

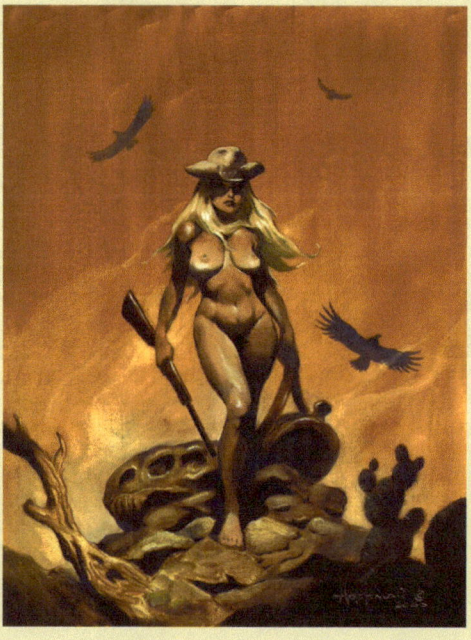

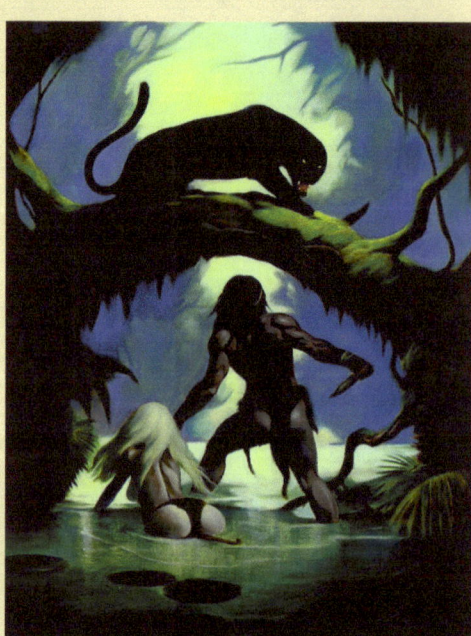

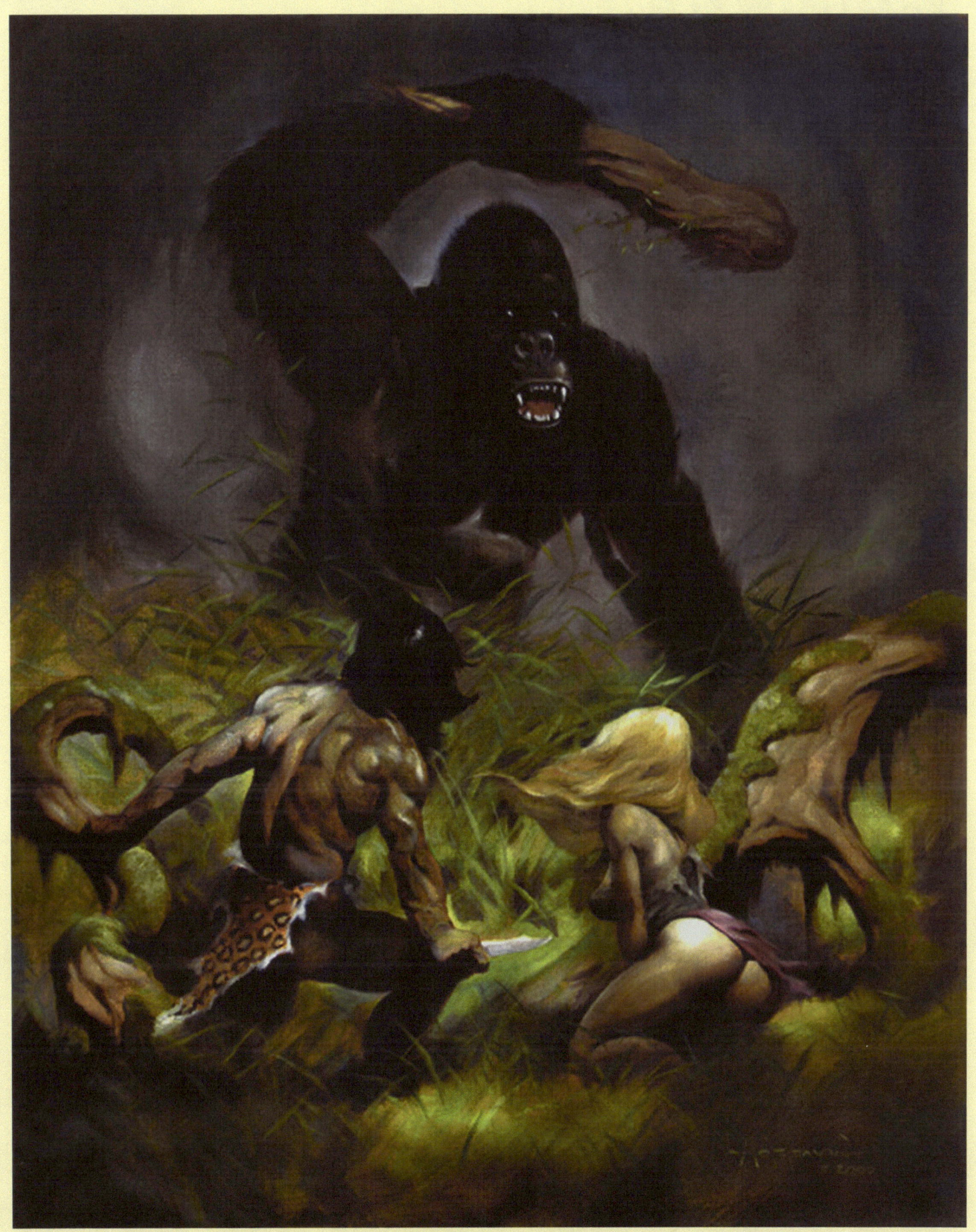

An attempt to strong-arm the Fantasy Art community via the intensity of blind ambition and energy realized in "The Giant Ape".

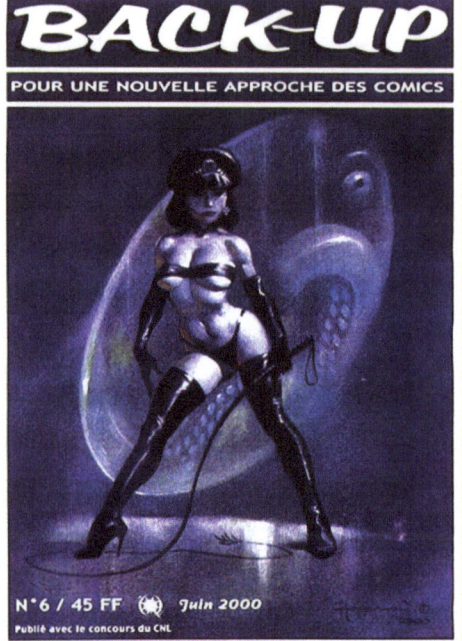

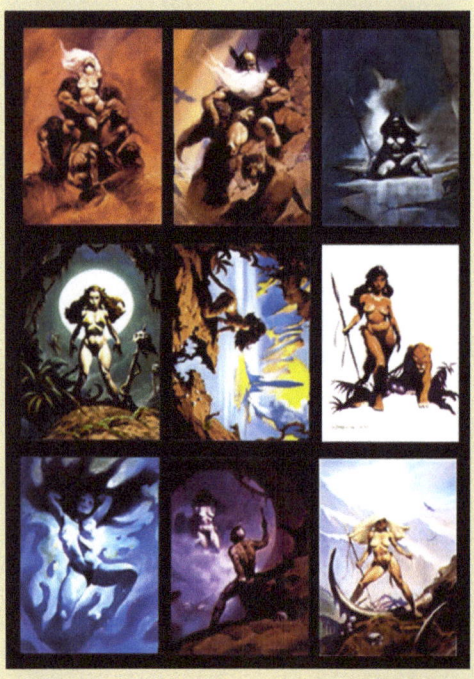

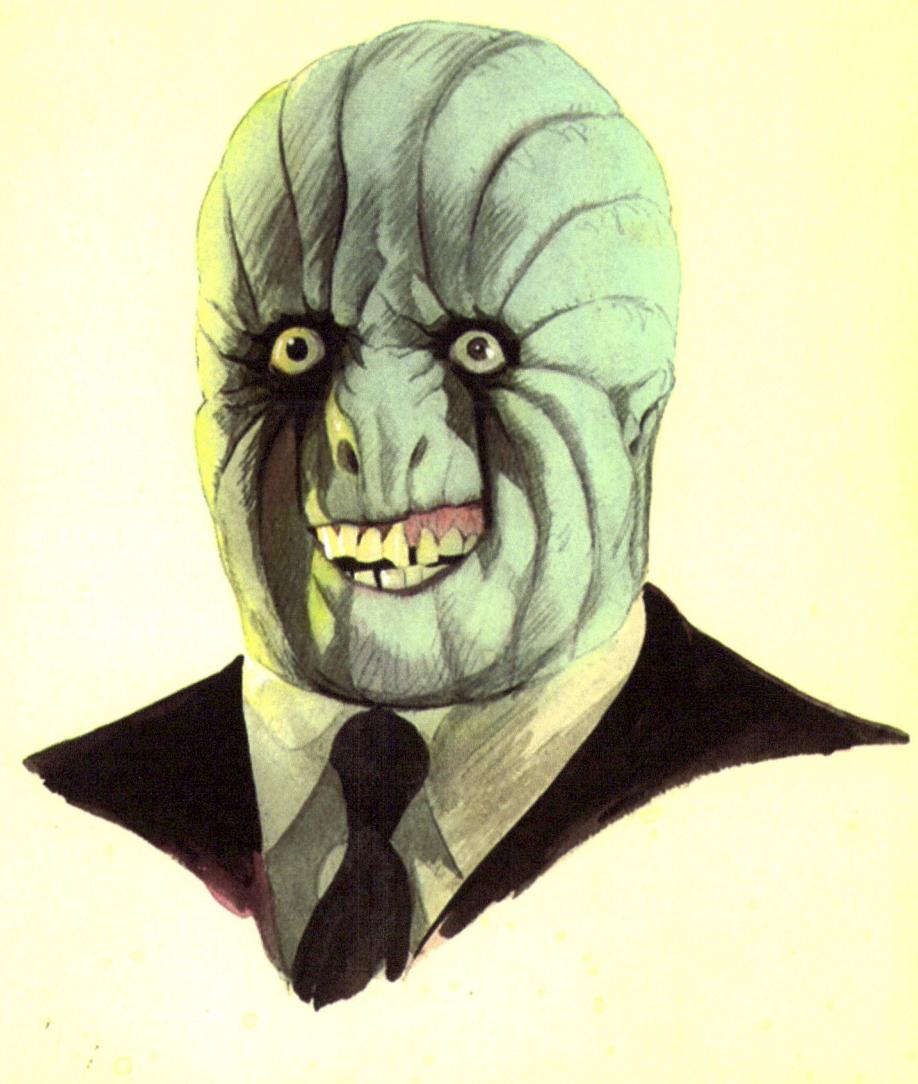

Odd works for publishers appeared, like the Hoffman-designed *Hellraiser* character *Pumpkinhead,* the French fanzine *Back-Up;* a Hoffman card set *Worlds of Wonder;* a few pieces catered to fan tastes, like *Black Widow, Flash Gordon,* and *Conan and Red Sonja.*

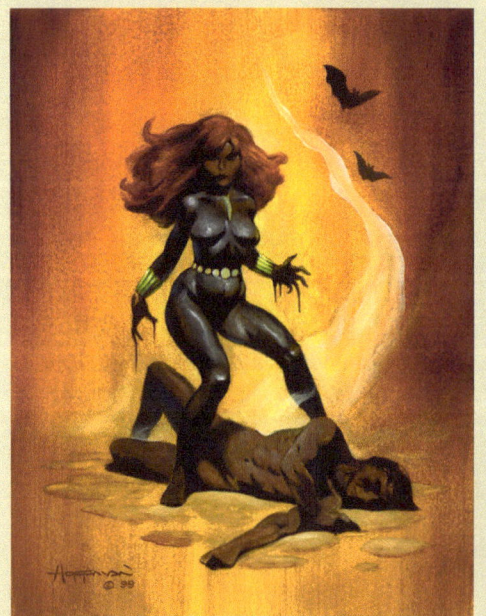

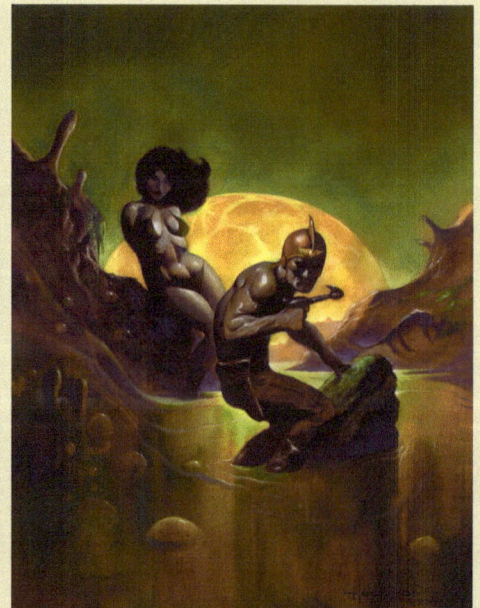

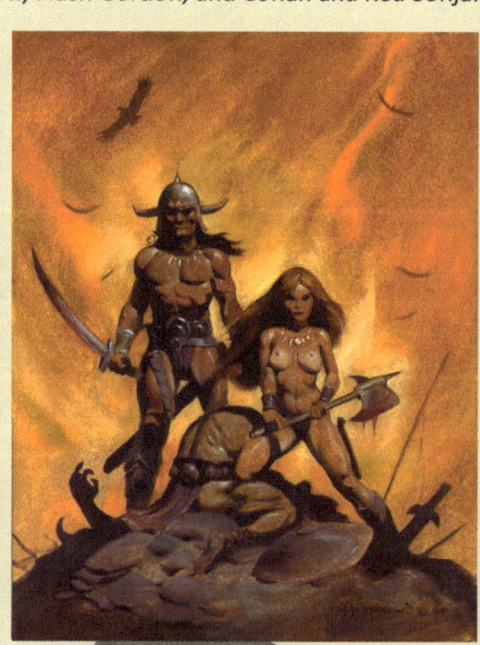

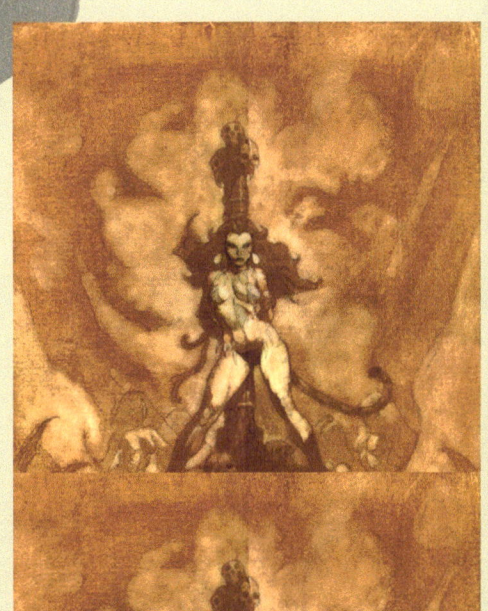

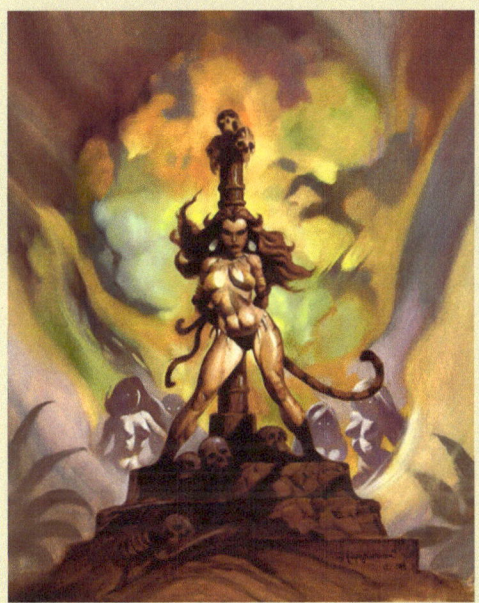

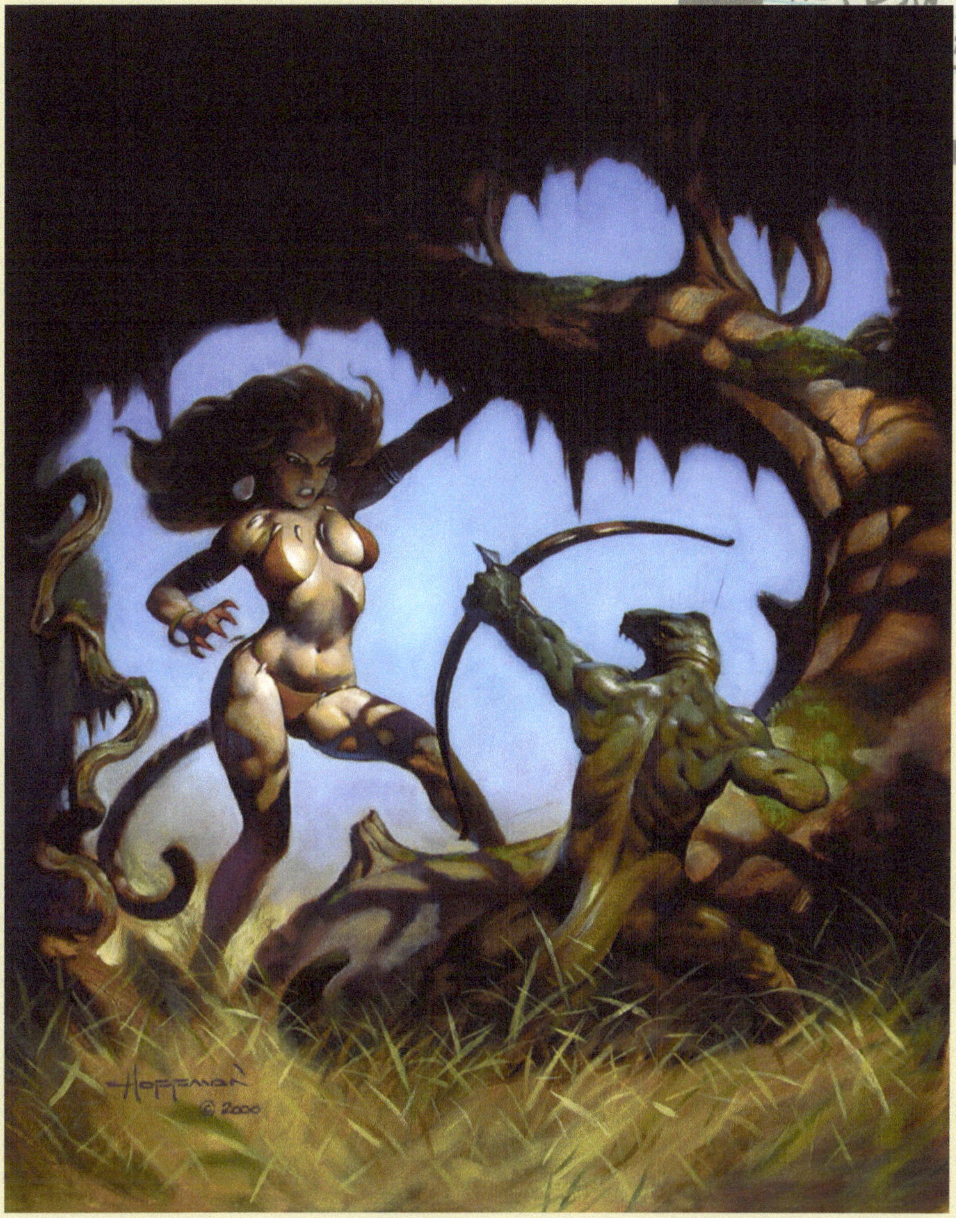

The original *Tigress Hunter* painting, above, was recently spotted for sale at a convention for $3,000; at left, the progression from underpainting to published version and then a later revised version; bottom, a first attempt at a *Tigress Bound* piece; the final cover.

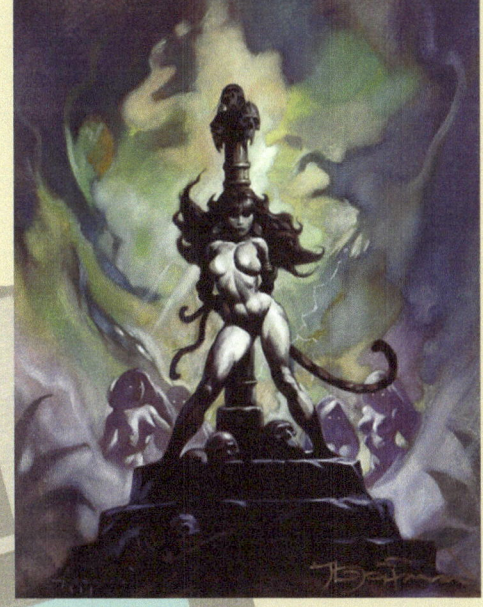

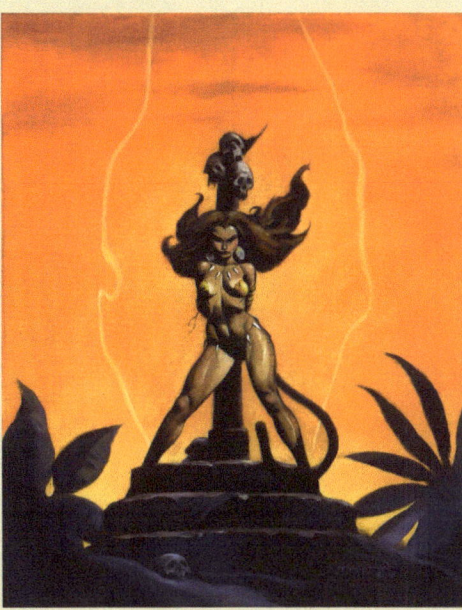

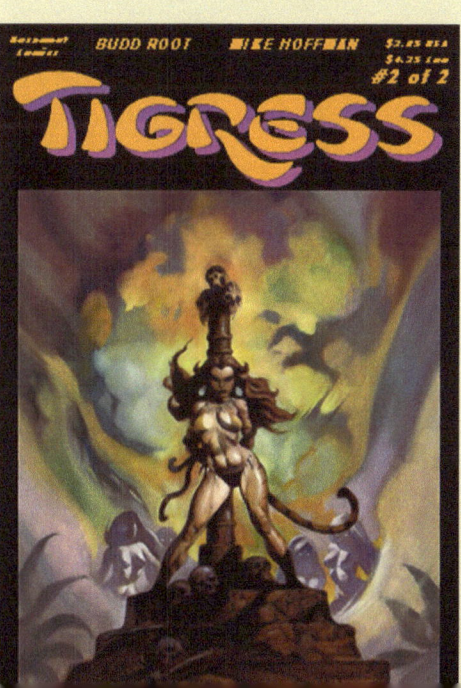

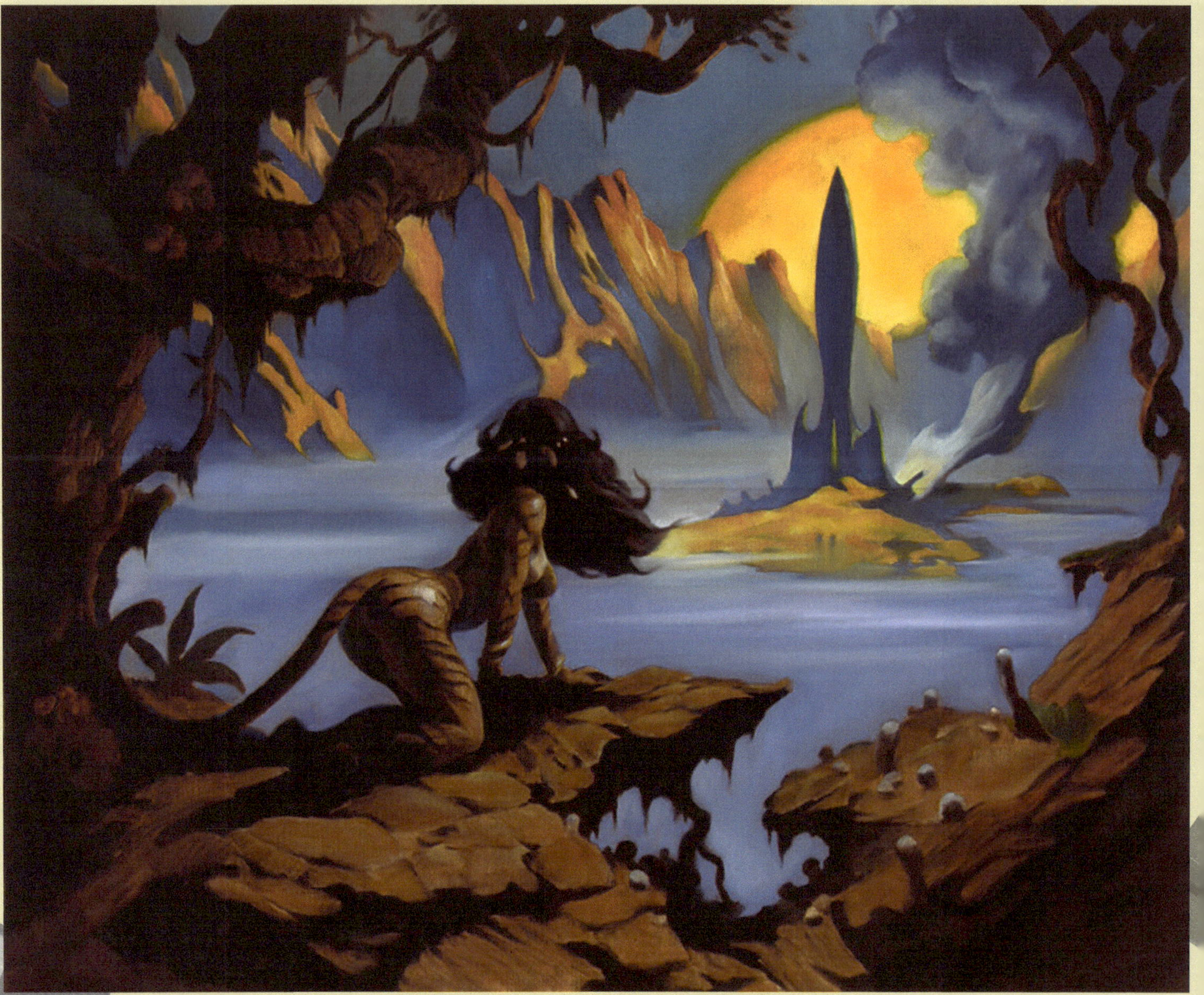

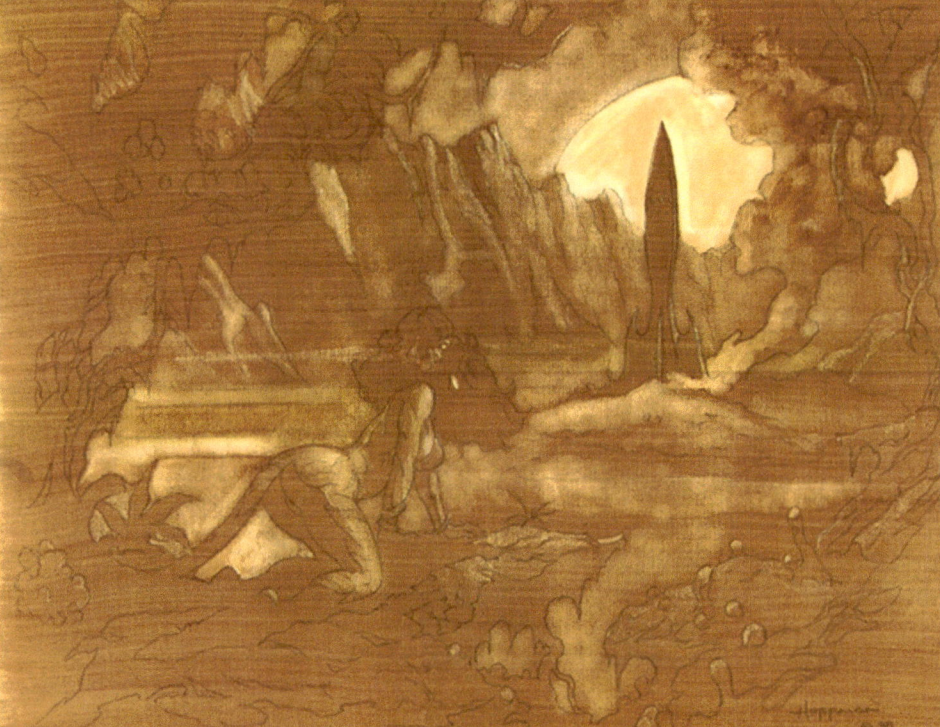

Above: a rare landscape-shaped painting *Tigress Planet* appeared on the back cover of the original *Tigress* series, issue #2; below left is the umber underpainting.

At bottom right is a Tigress pin-up created to fill leftover pages in the 32-page comic; the series attracted a healthy readership for a time, then with the name change to *Tigress Tales* and inclusion of other material, sales waned. Eventually, the Tigress character appeared only in "one-shot" single issue stories with self-contained storylines.

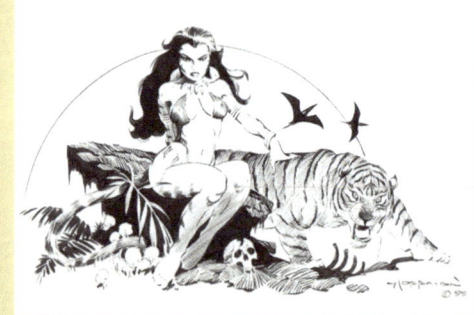

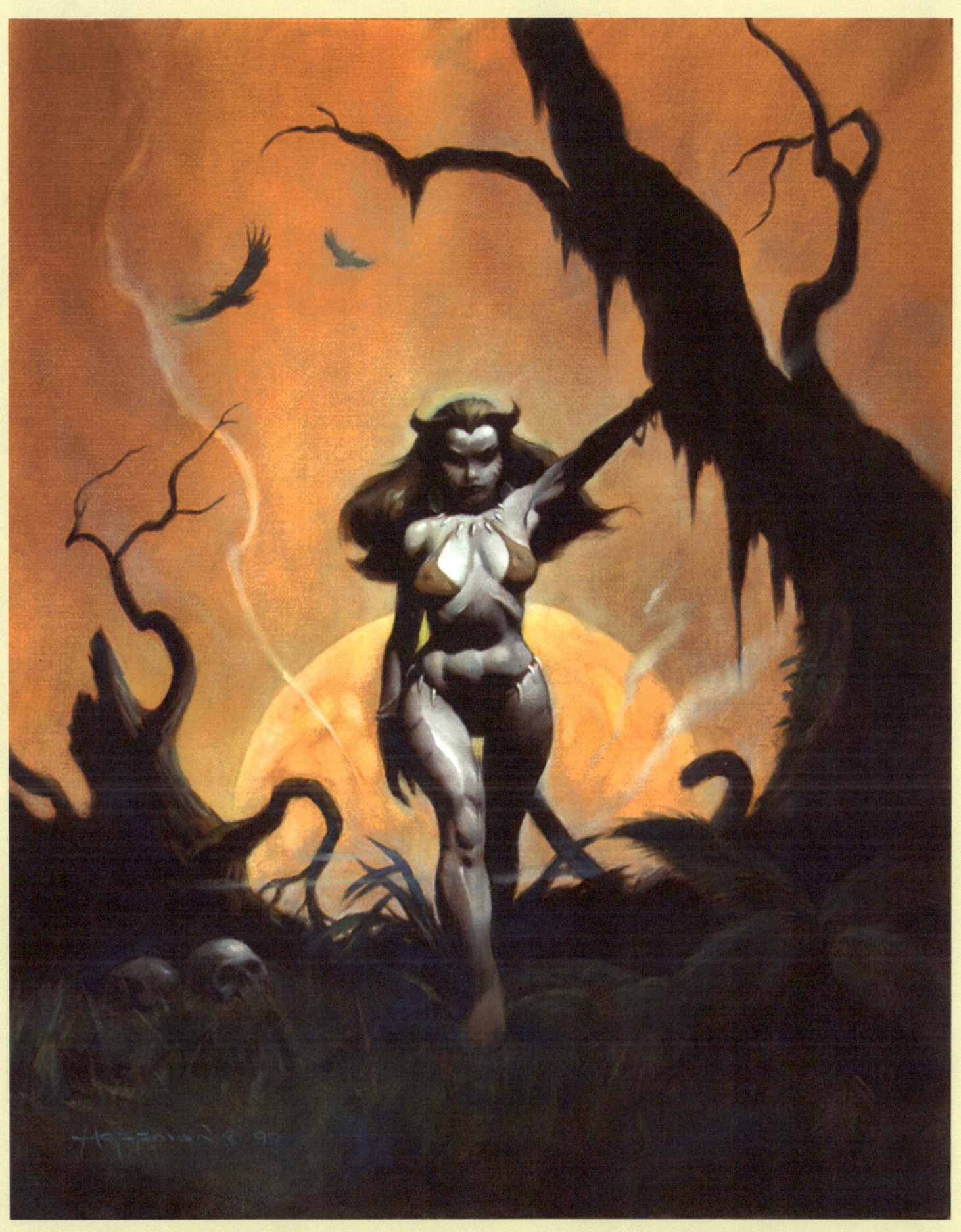

A Tigress portrait titled "Tigress Planet", painted for pleasure in 2000 and printed in the art book "Sorceress II".

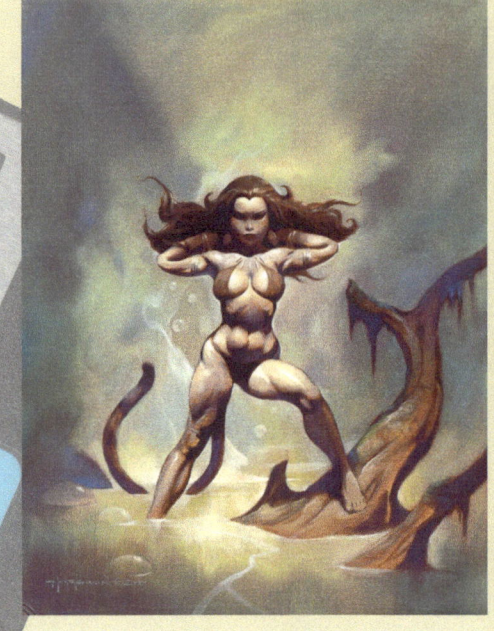

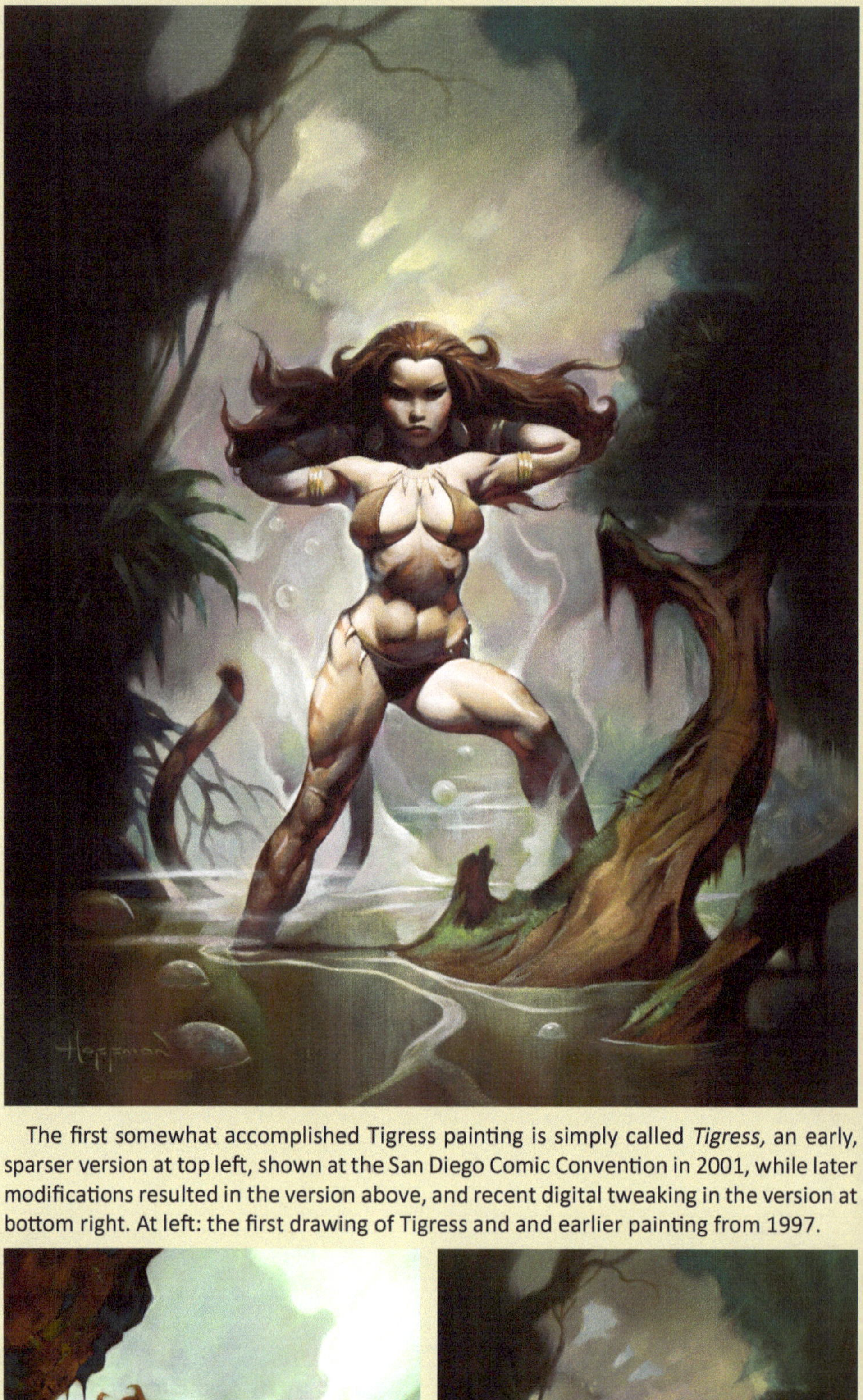

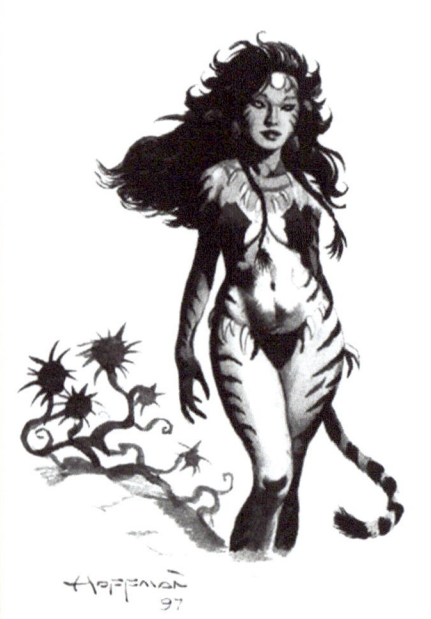

The first somewhat accomplished Tigress painting is simply called *Tigress,* an early, sparser version at top left, shown at the San Diego Comic Convention in 2001, while later modifications resulted in the version above, and recent digital tweaking in the version at bottom right. At left: the first drawing of Tigress and and earlier painting from 1997.

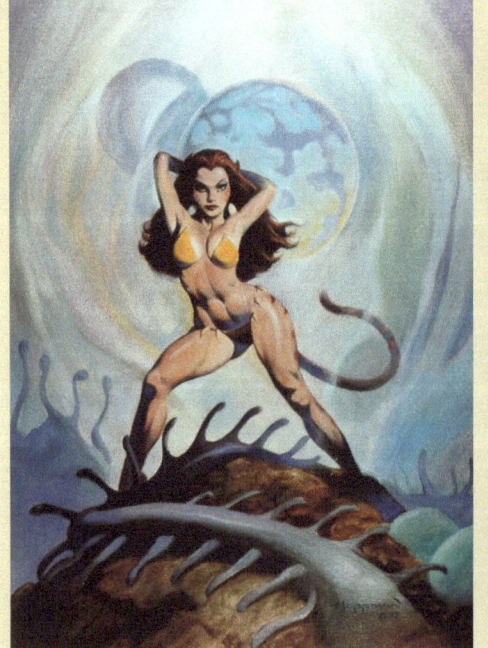

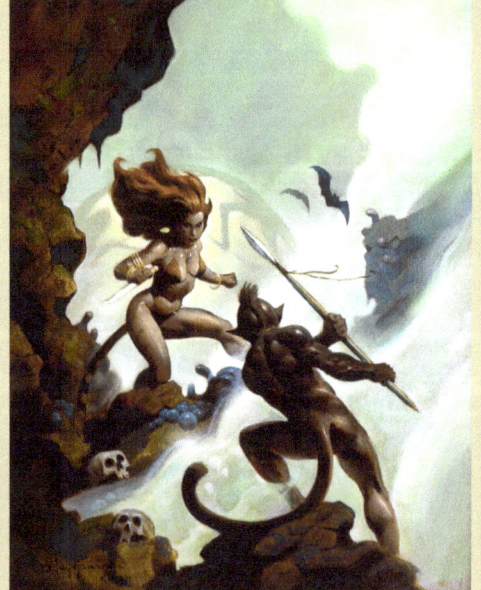

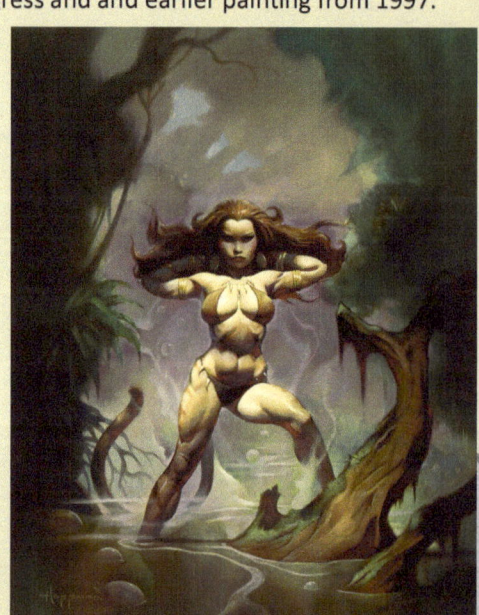

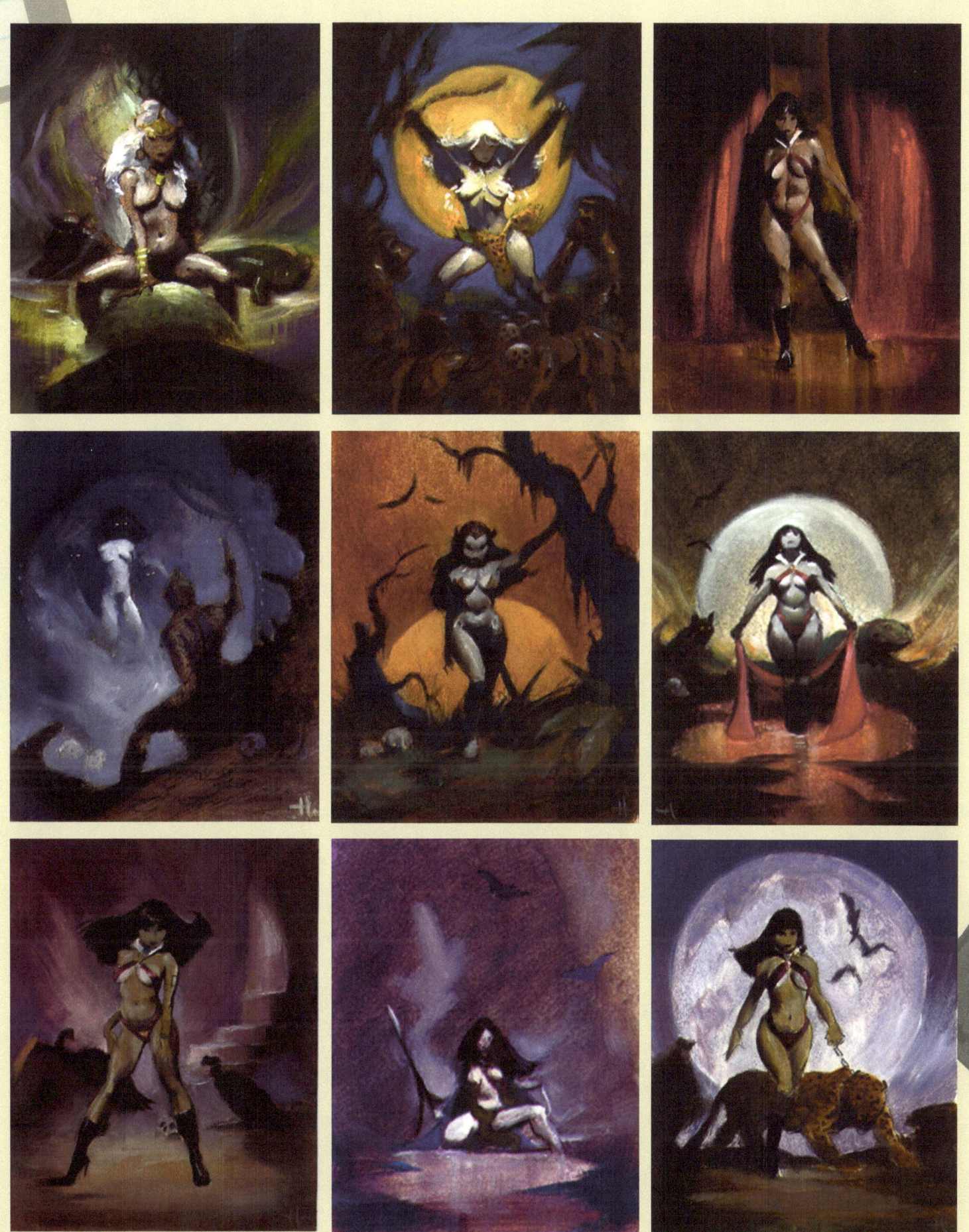

A selection of small, 4x5 inch oil roughs on heavy illustration board, many of which were turned into paintings included in this book.

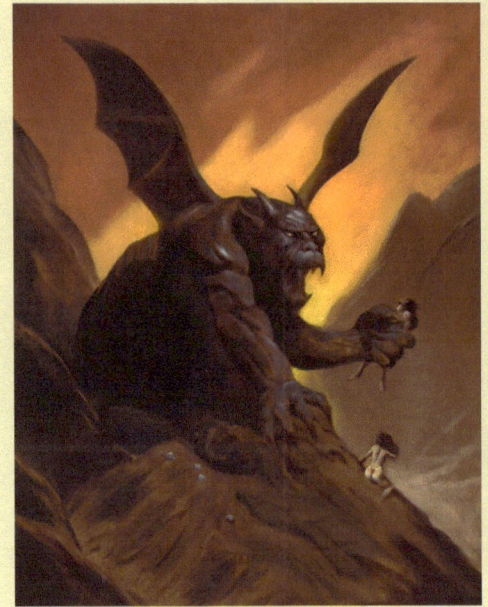

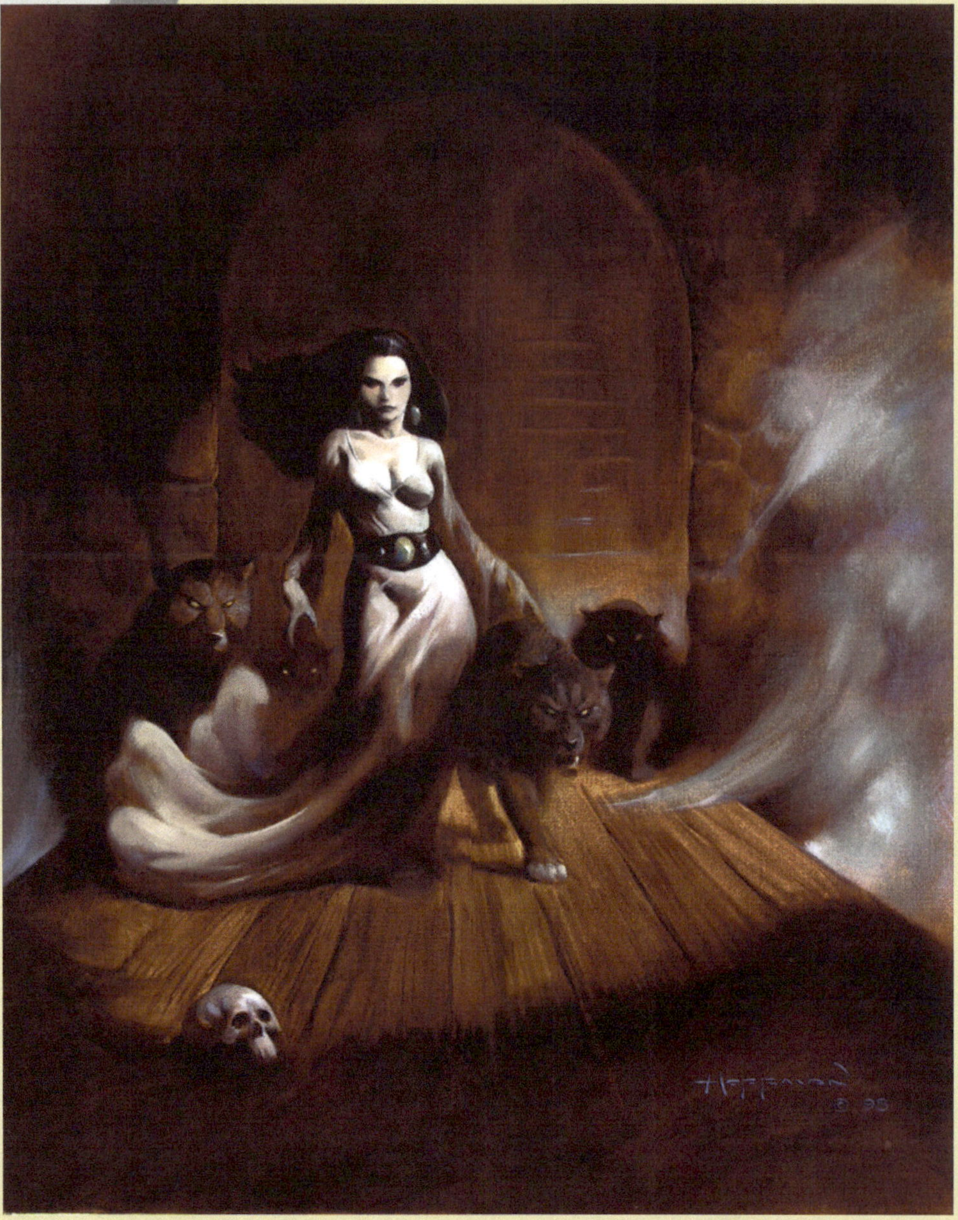

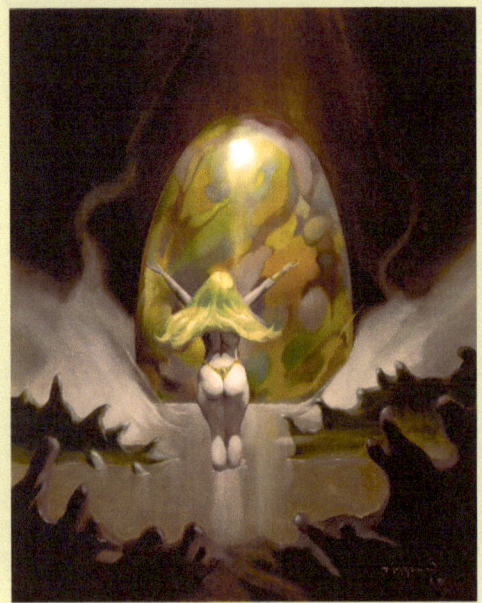

Various pre-2000 paintings were produced for *Troll Magazine,* who requested speed, never paid, and had the gall to send a "confidentiality contract" about the affair. *Wolf-girl,* above; left, *Gargoyle Mountain, Gem Girl, Gargoyle Burster;* below, *Nucklavee,* a half-horse-half-human mythical being; *Jungle Girl,* sold but lost in the Postal system.

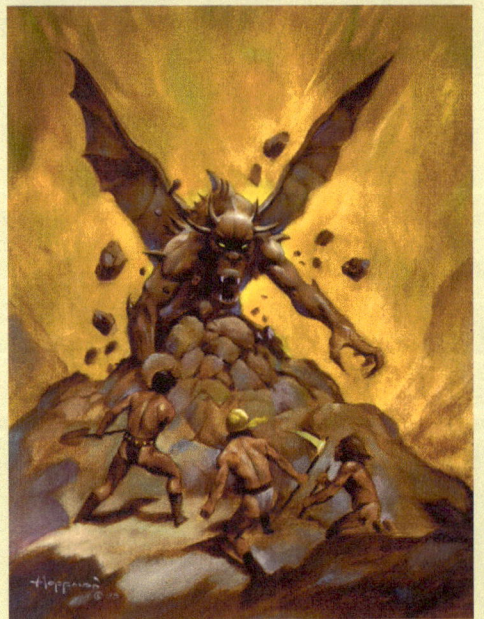

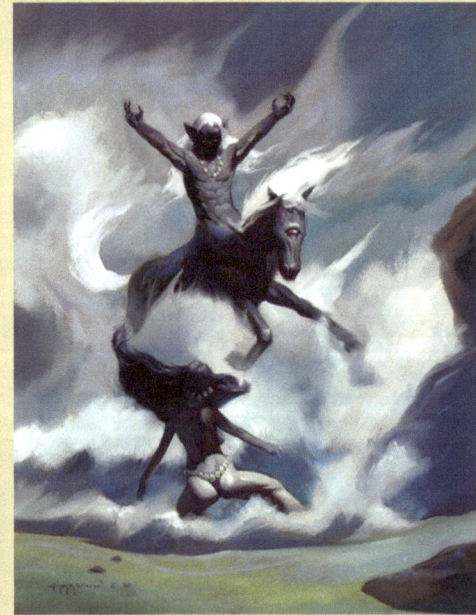

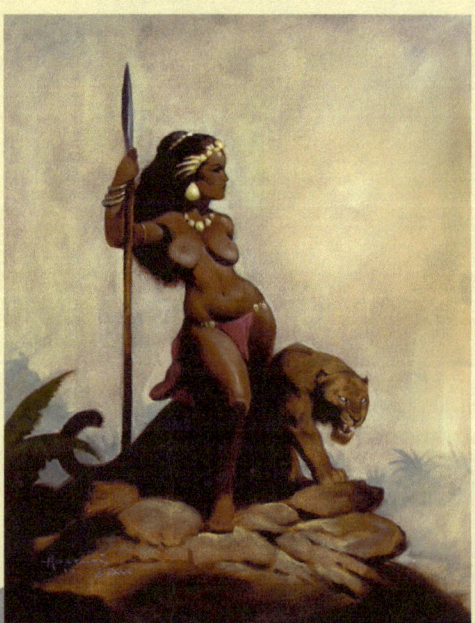

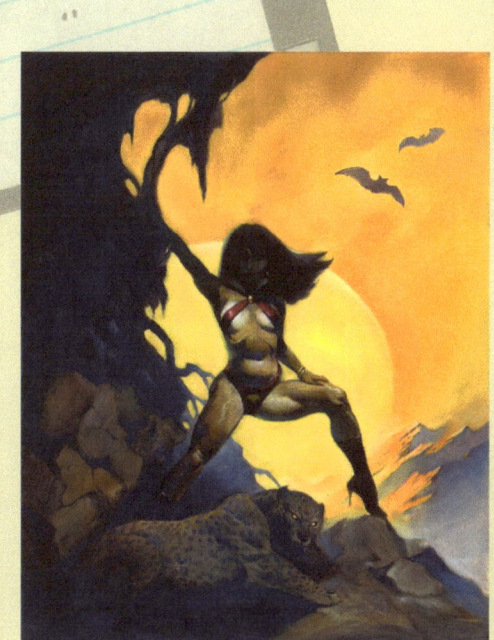

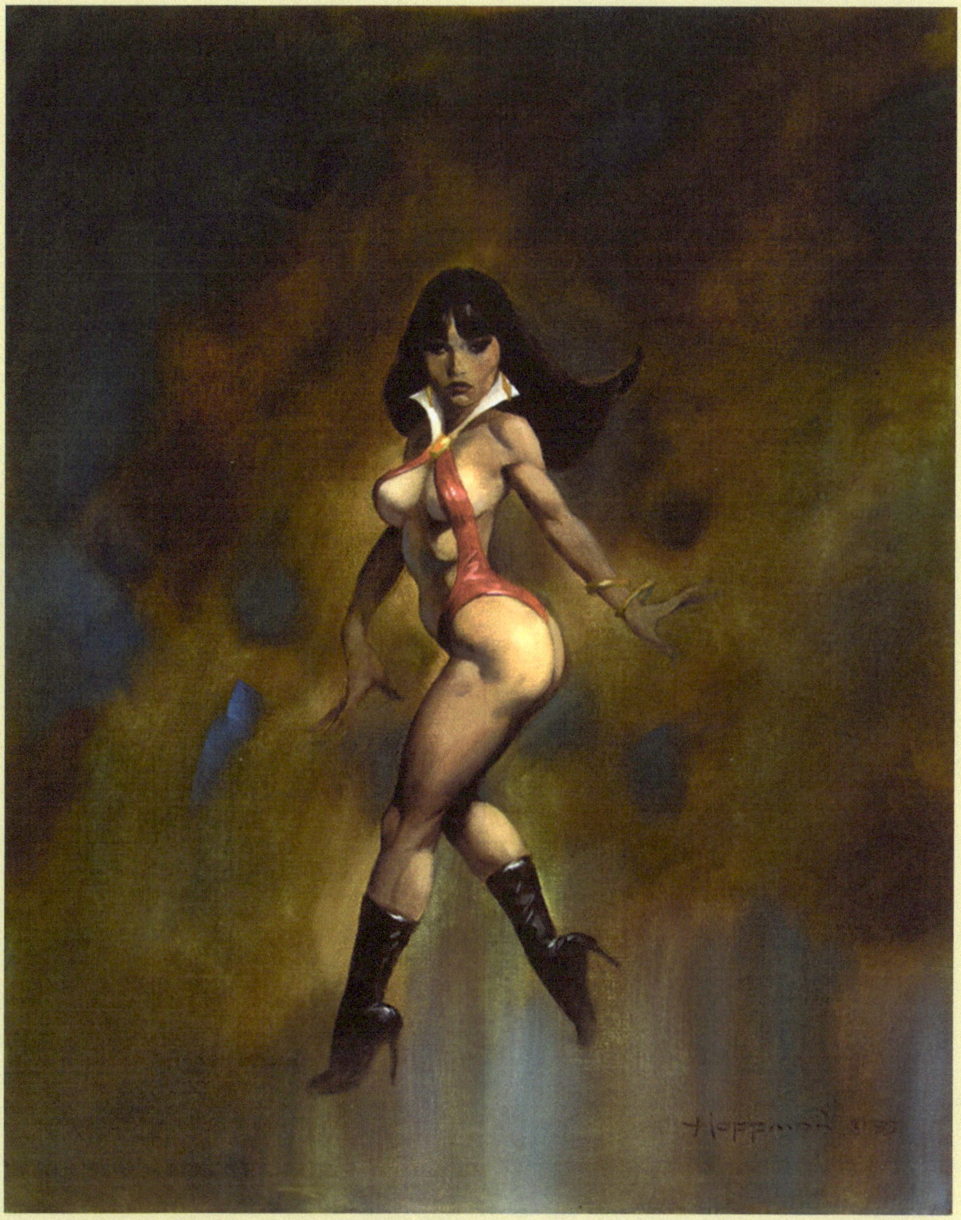

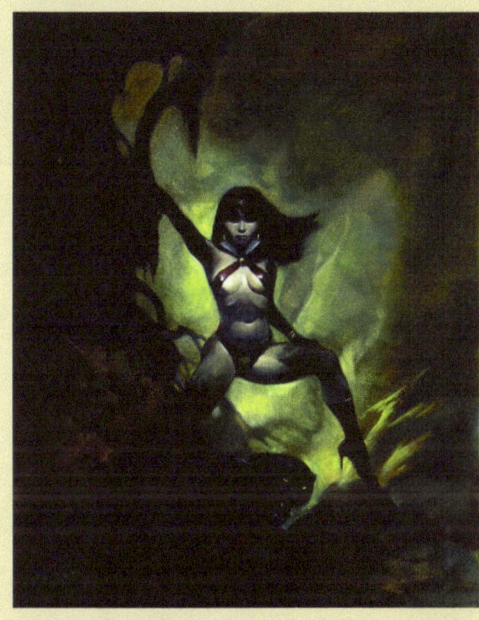

Vampirella might well be the Comic artist's greatest curse; draw or paint her well, and you'll likely be asked for nothing but; fail to render her well, and you may starve. Above: *Vampi Dancer,* left row: two stages of *Jungle Vampi,* below *Vampi Leopard* & *Swamp.*

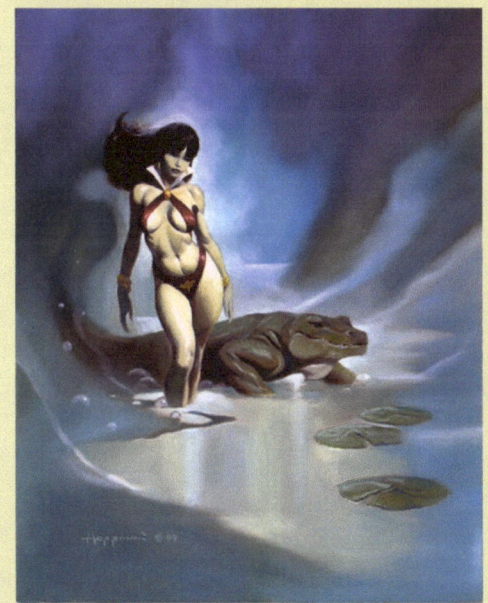

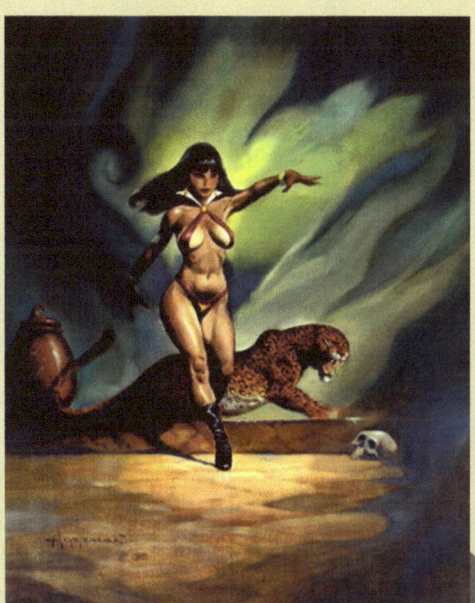

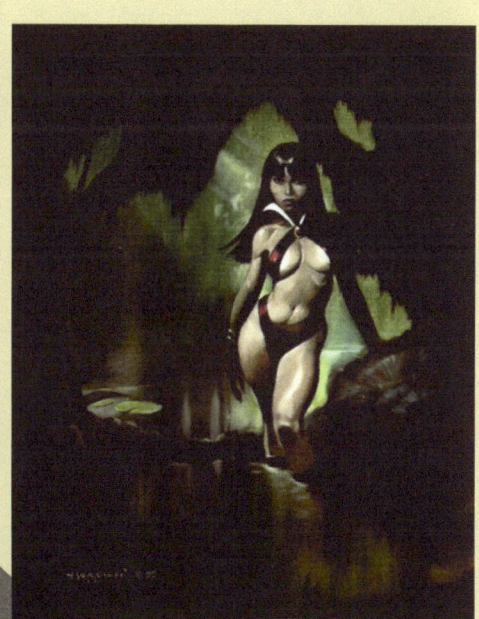

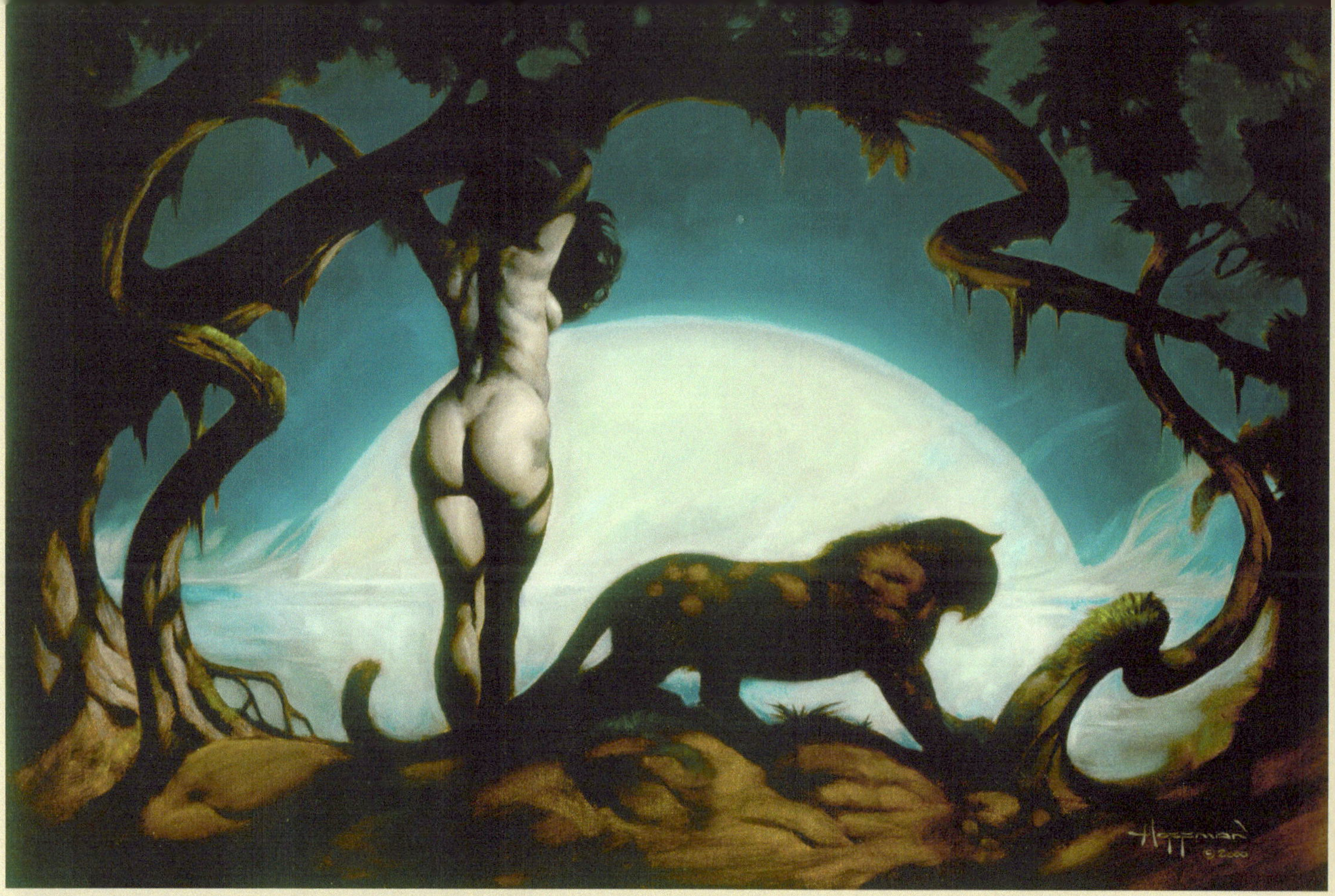

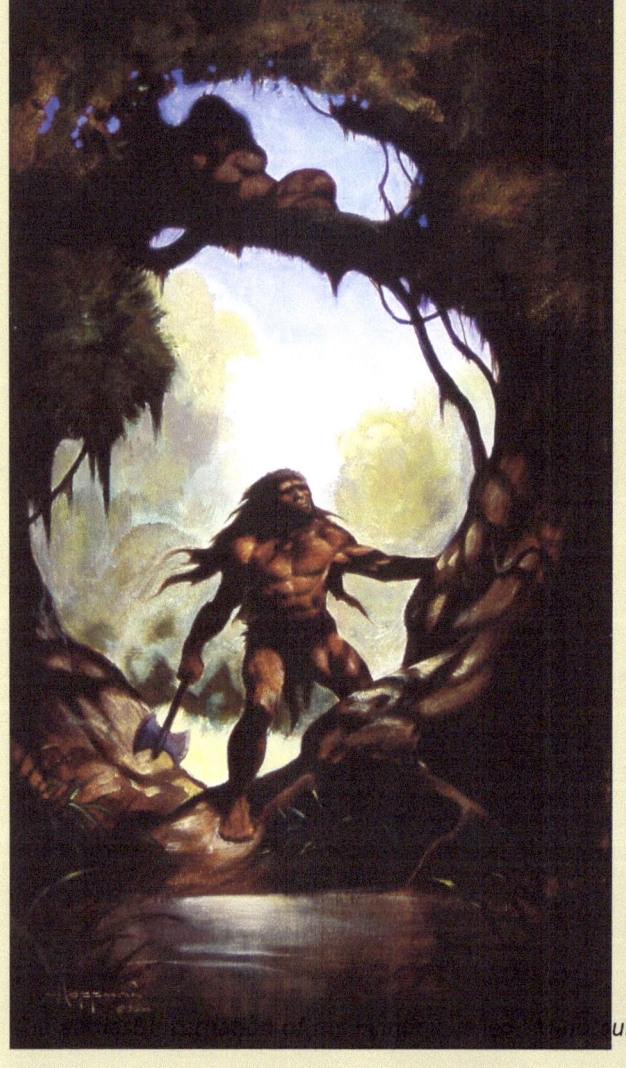

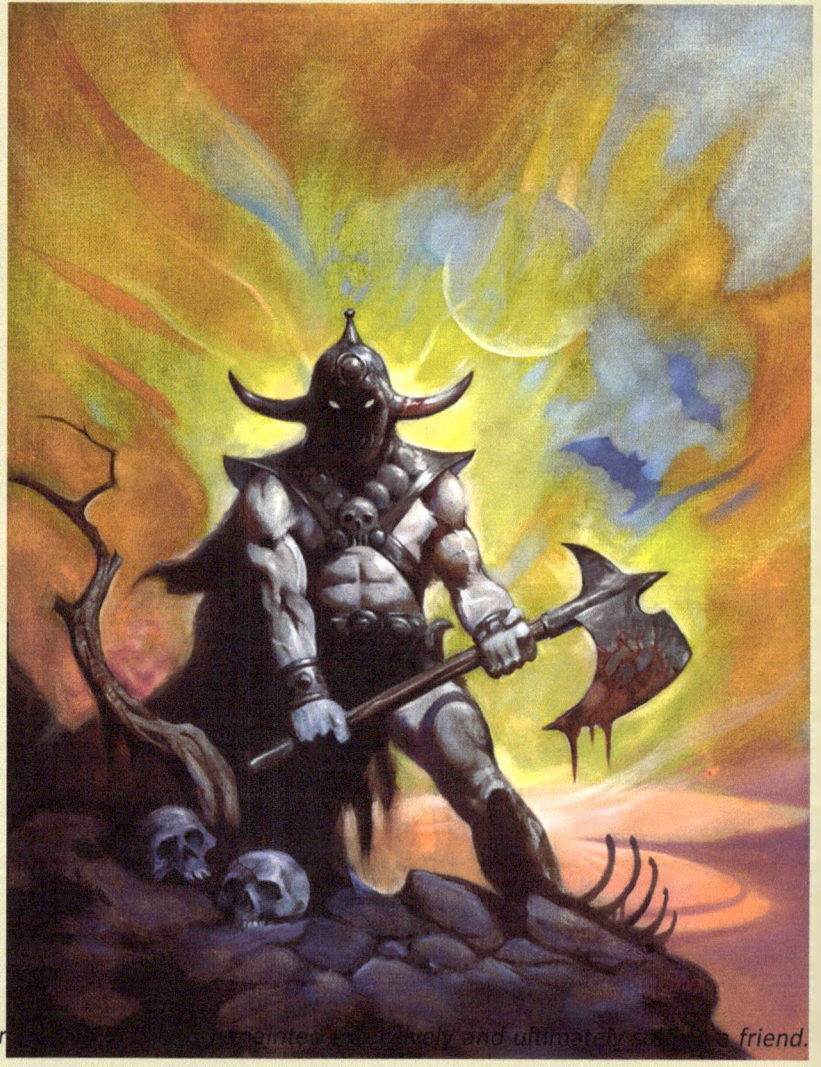

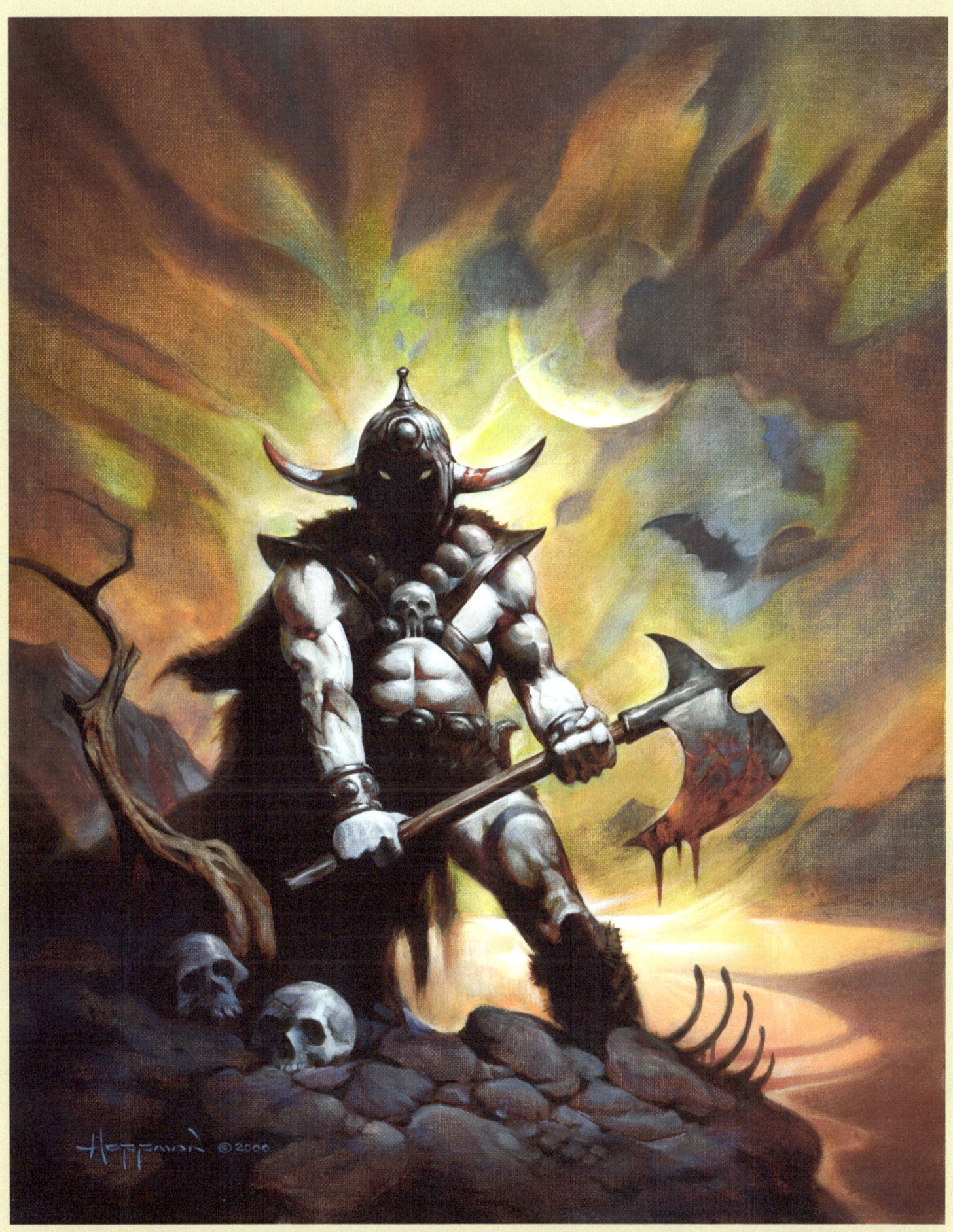

Above: *Minotaur,* being pushed away from a "color" emphasis towards light and value (compare to previous version on preceding page), preceding page, top and left: the large commissioned works *Jungle Planet* and *Hunted,* both painted on raw canvas adhered to masonite.

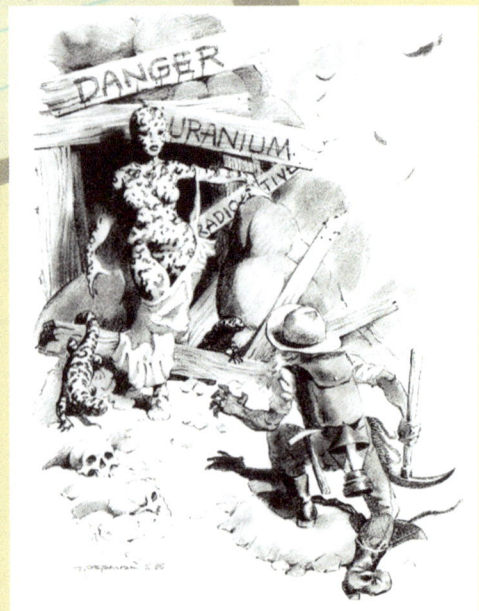

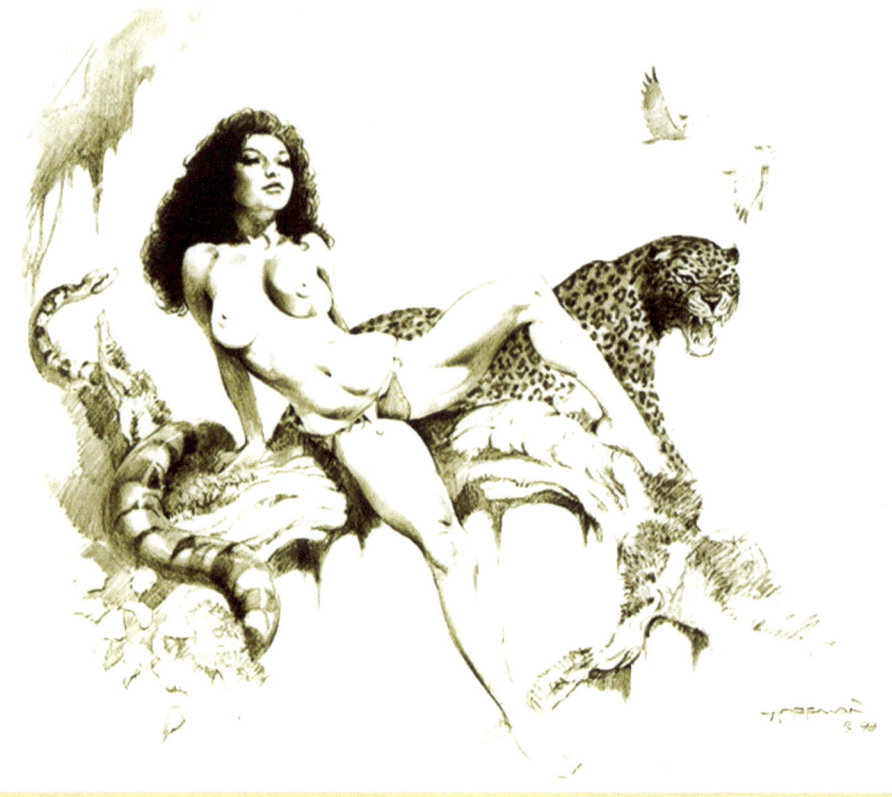

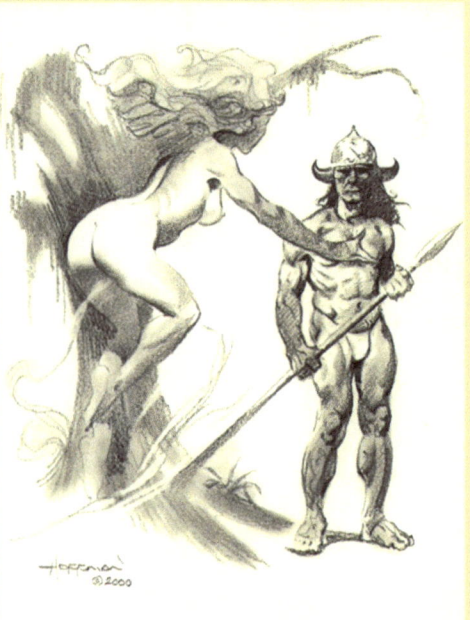

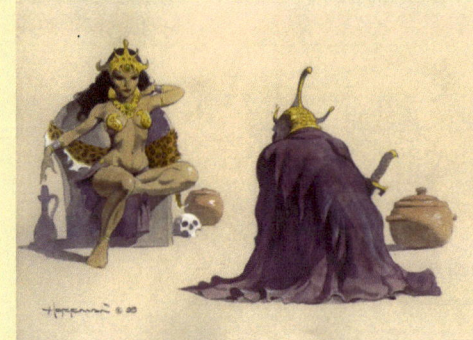

I produced many, many $50 pencil drawings for SQP's myriad erotic pinup books, and those original drawings have been held by the publisher ever since and may still surface on the market again someday.

This page features typical monster and big cat artworks, and a watercolored drawing on *Stonehenge Gray* paper, which I found in an Art store but no longer use; it was grayish but with a warm tint.

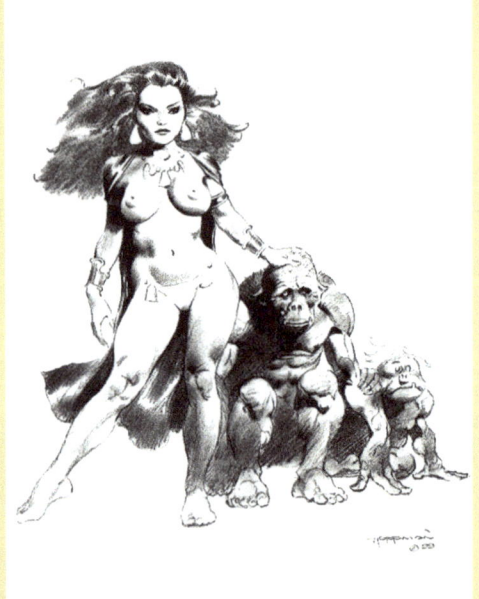

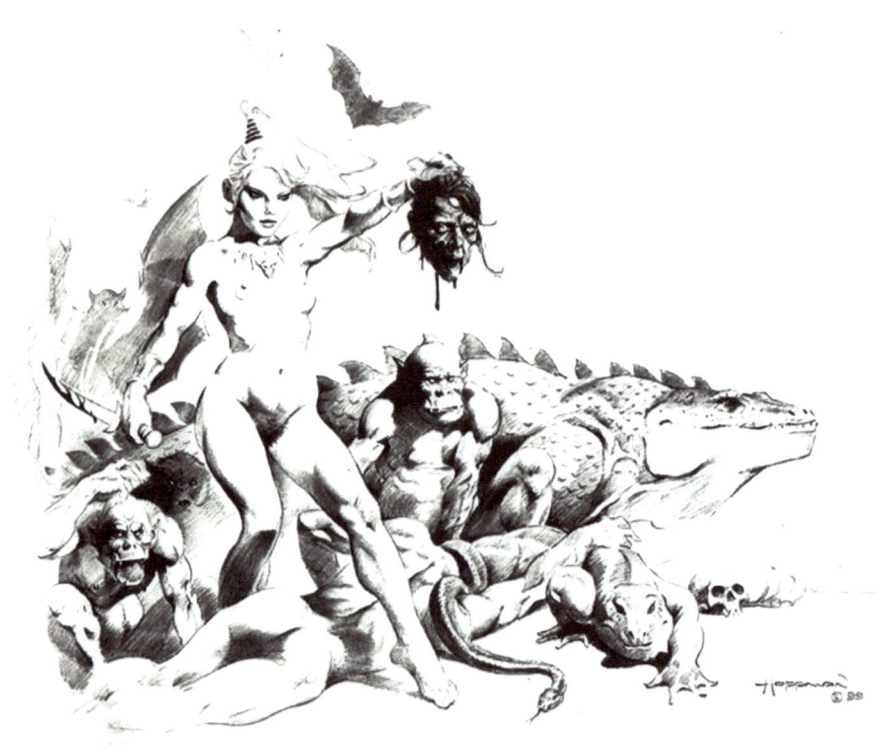

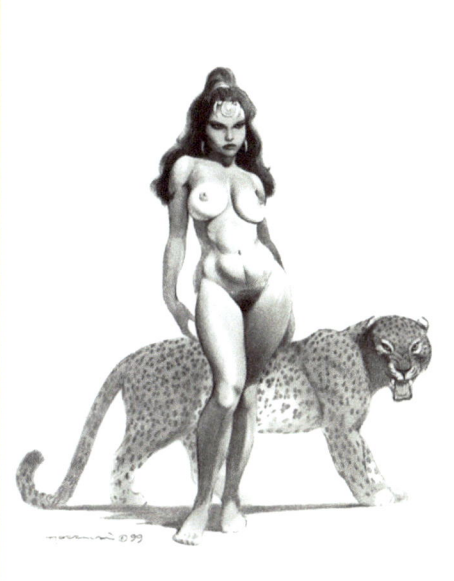

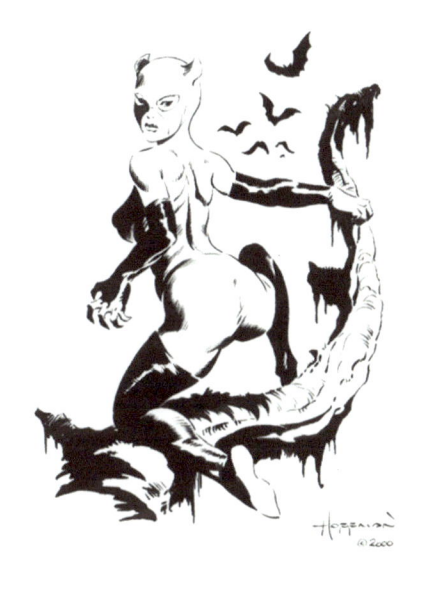

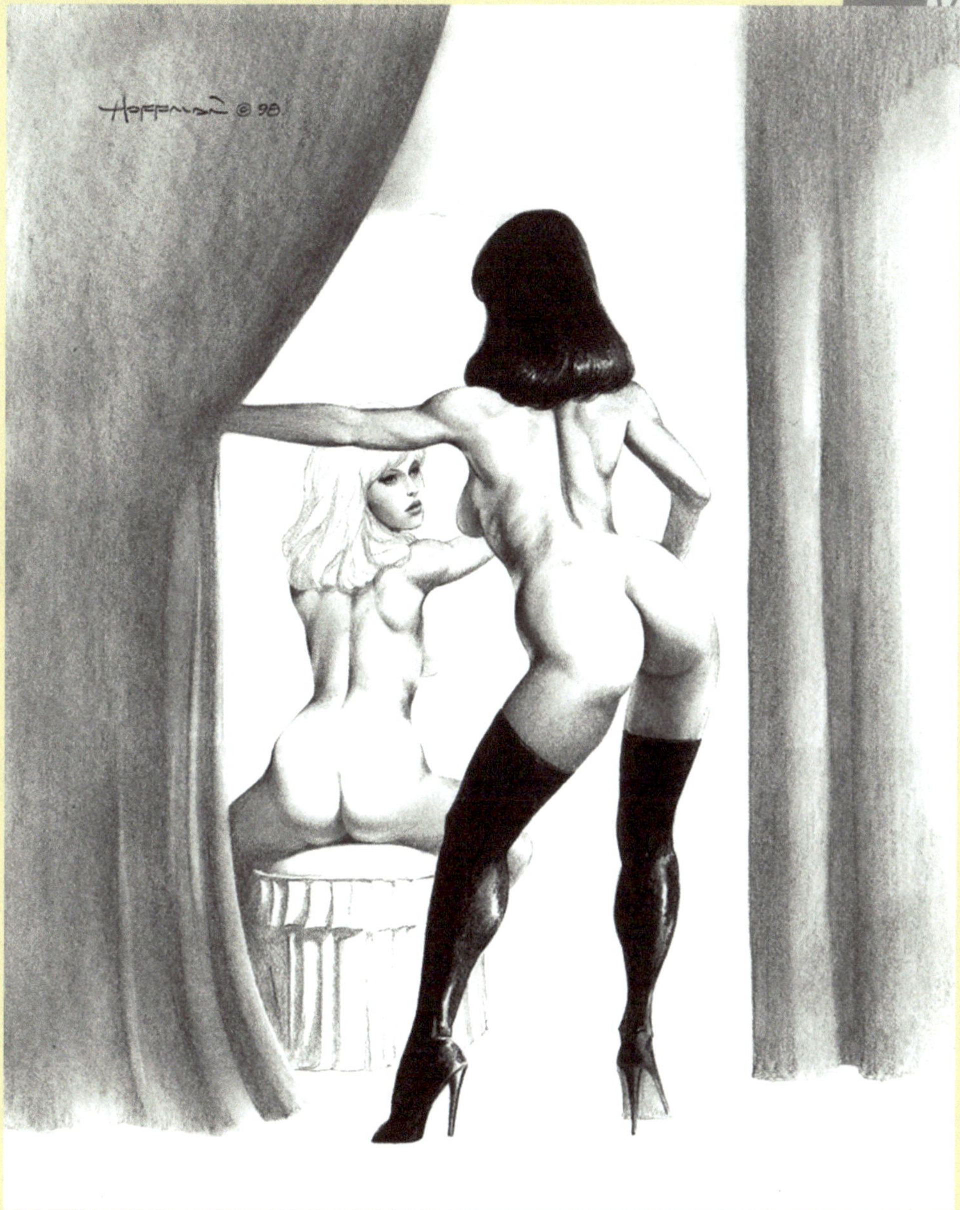

Unsurprisingly, erotic ideas played well to fans and sold books for publishers and originals for the artist, the above drawing for SQPs *Leather & Lace,* others for the public.

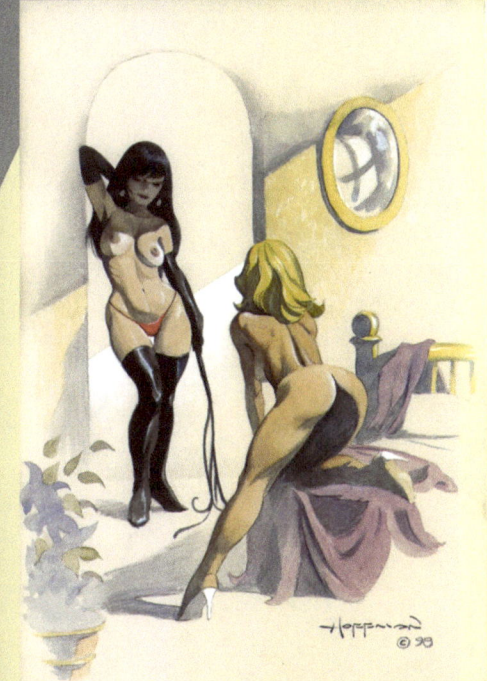

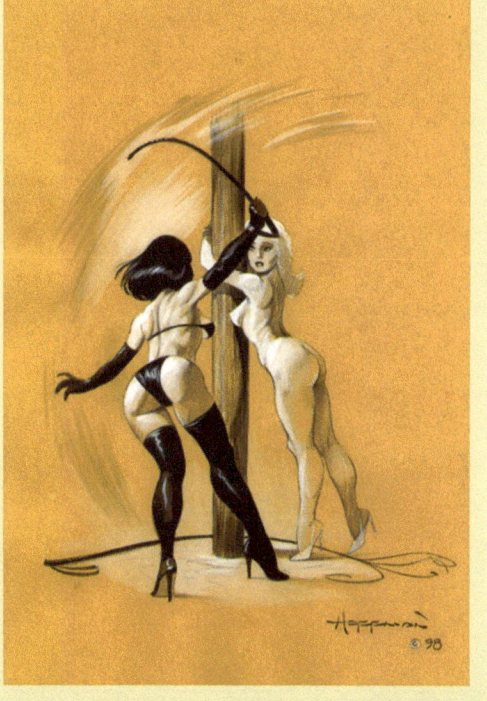

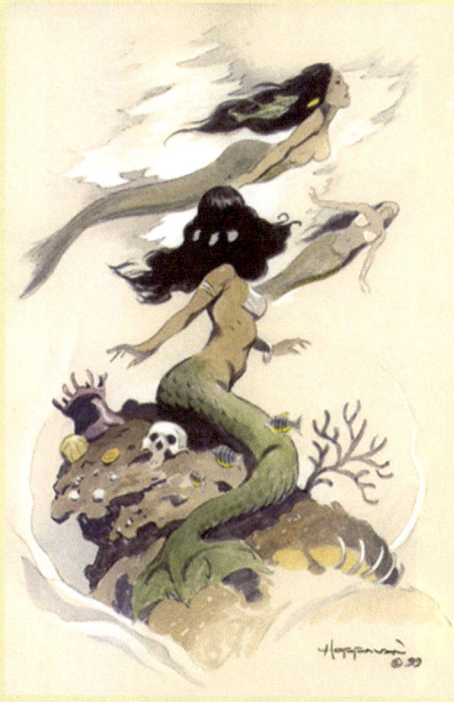

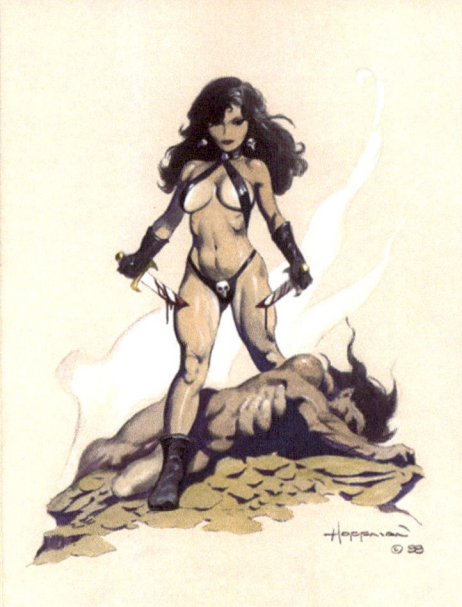

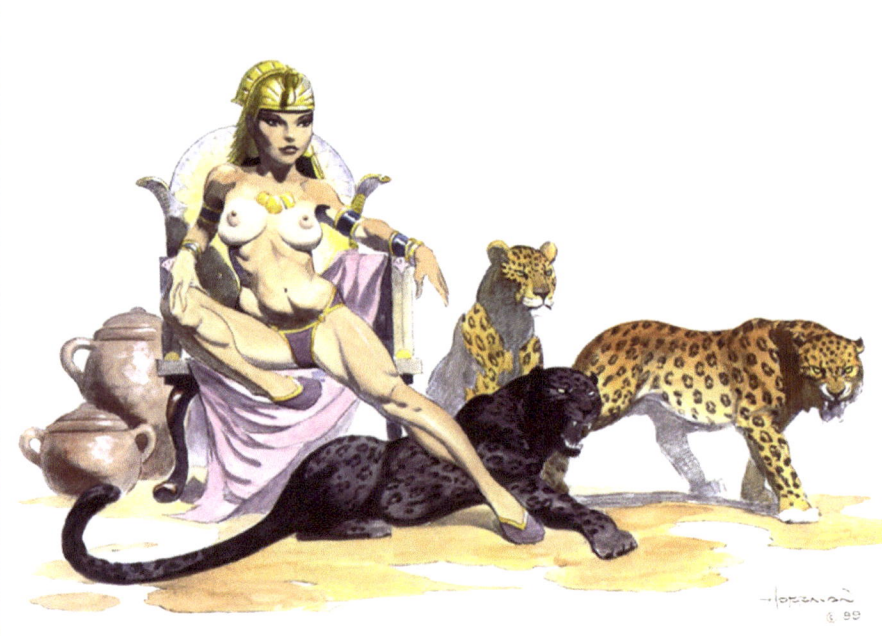

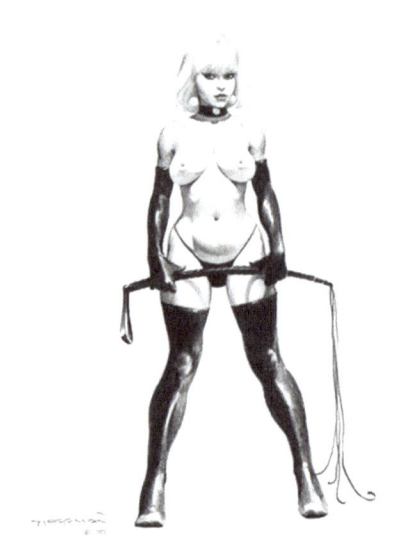

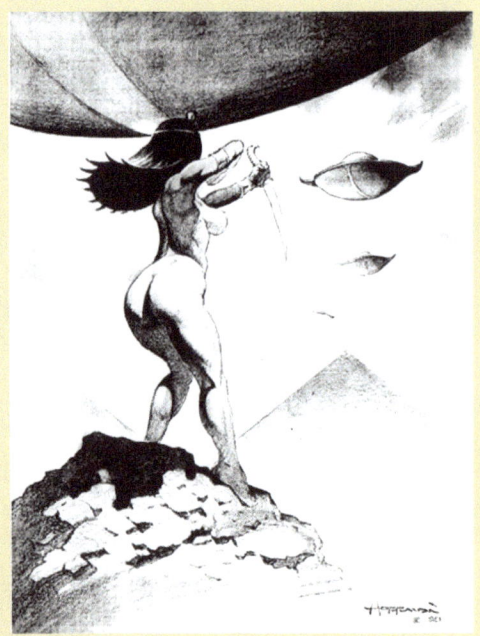

1997 was so distant from today that at that time comic artists were still communicating with publishers by telephone and hastily-assembled xerox copies made at the local office shop. Slightly earlier still, there was no email for average people, and the PC was still conspicuously absent from most homes.

This page features more SQP drawings, some with an Egyptian theme for the book titled *Eternal Temptation*, like the one immediately left called *The Builders;* left of it is Dominatrix, below Ivory Queen, bottom center *Cleopatra*, right corner, *Biker Trash*.

At top left is a character I invented called "Bayonette", in the hopes of cashing in on the then-popular "Bad Girl" craze in Comics.

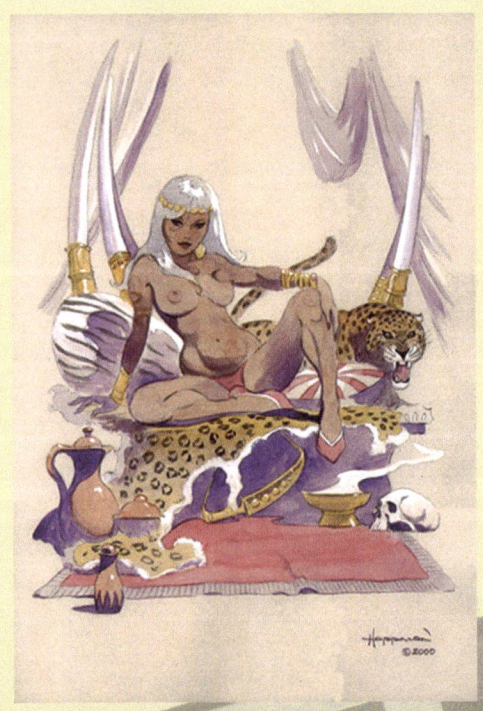

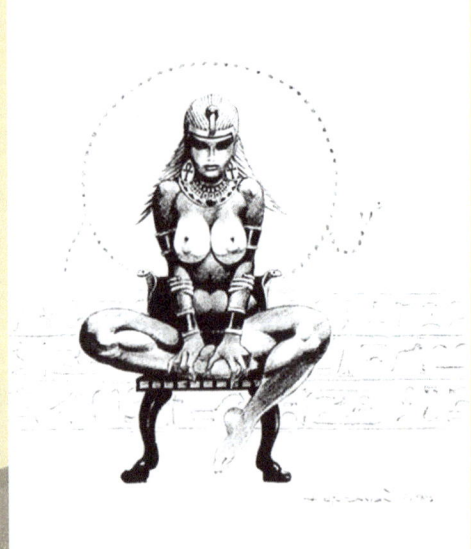

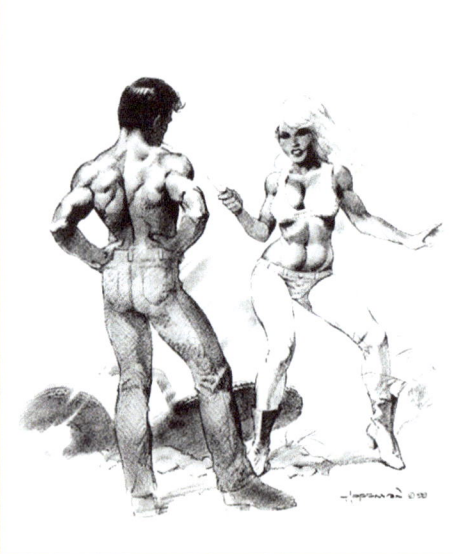

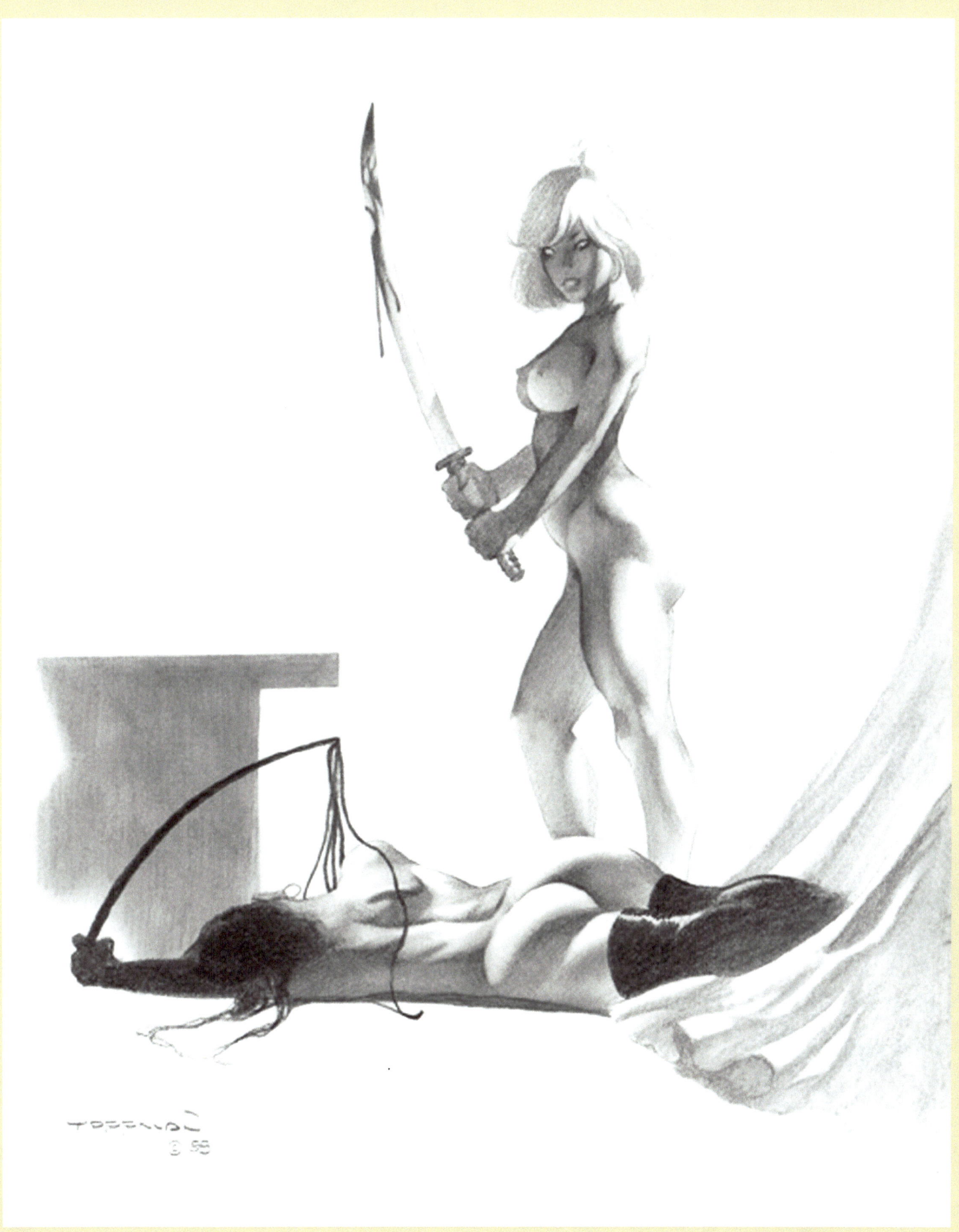

One of many erotic drawings produced for the art-hungry publisher SQP. Drawings from this era were don with mechanical pencils, in retrospect an absurdly effort-intensive approach. The popularity of "Revenge" has been constant over time.

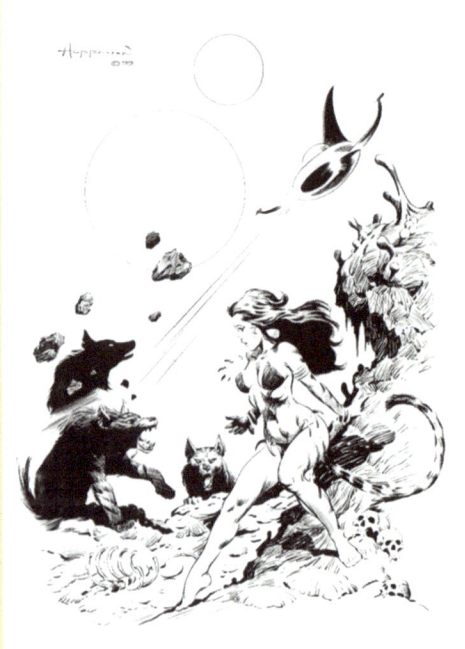

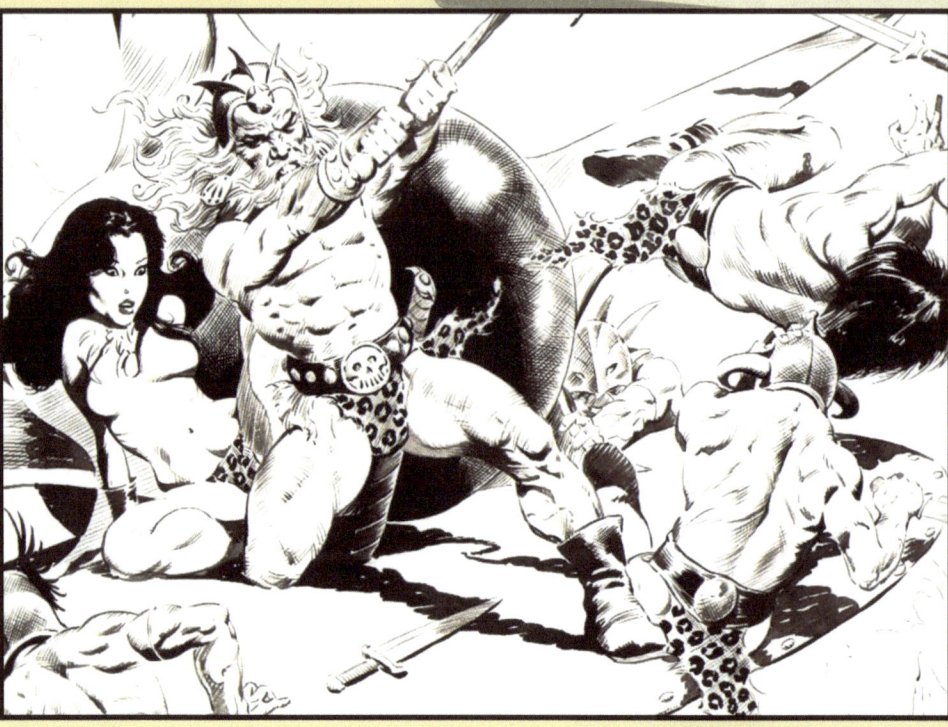

Drawings from the Floppy Age are somehow less "presentable" to me now, I suppose that painting in shapes lends some weight to the work that only outline can't adequately convey, and any shortcomings in drawing come to the fore.

Unsurprisingly, many top "Fantasy" artists paint acceptably but are somewhat weak in the draughtsmanship for the very same reason.

Above is a detail from *Space Berserker*, originally created for *SOD* Magazine; at bottom left is a drawing that appeared in the first *Tigress* comic, and later as a T-shirt design; the other two pieces were pinups also published in the *Tigress* comics.

Hoffman

TIGRESS

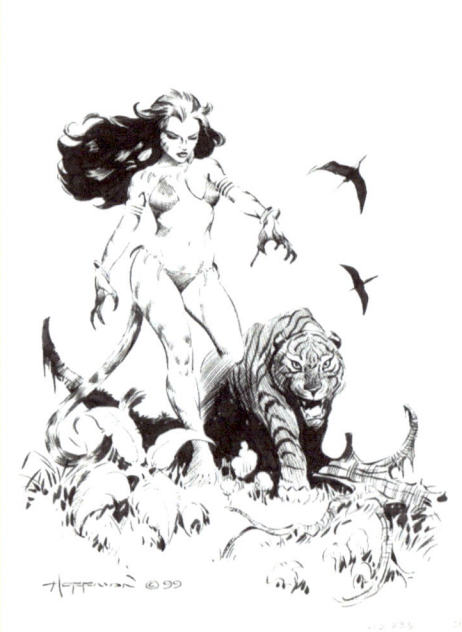

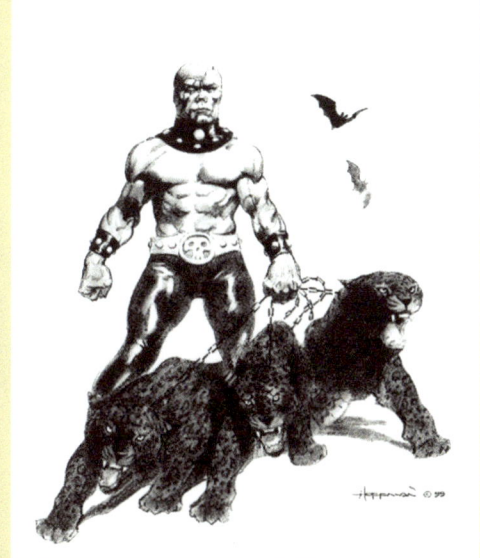

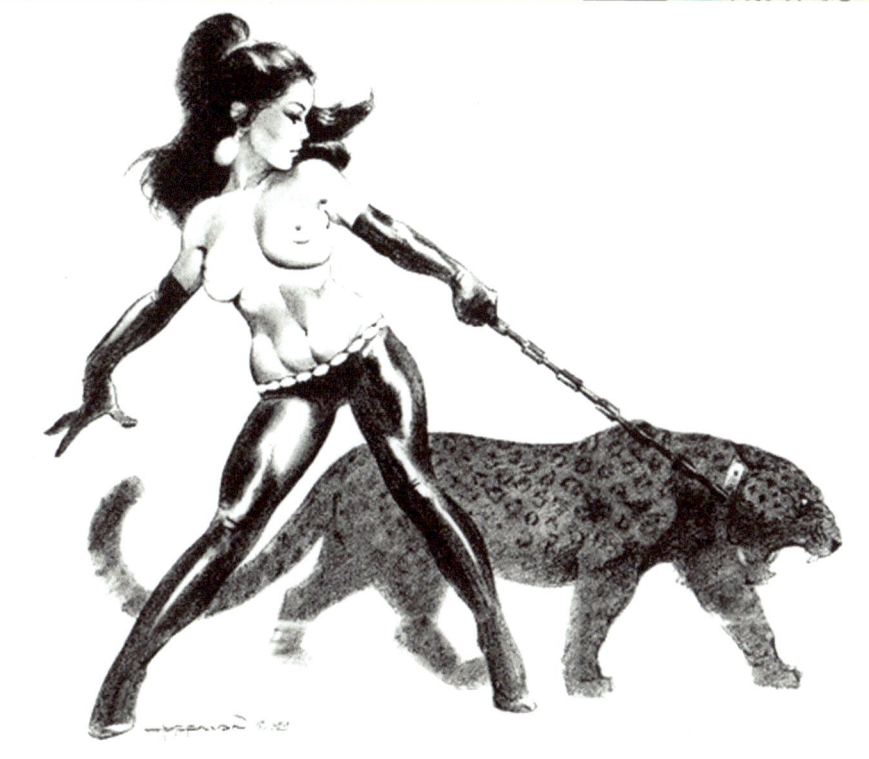

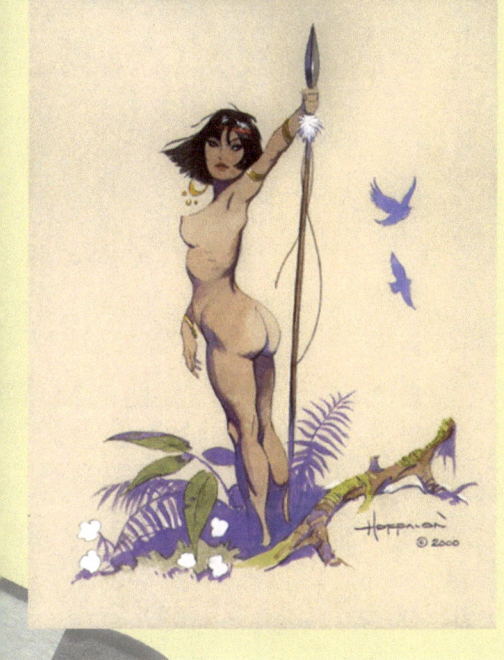

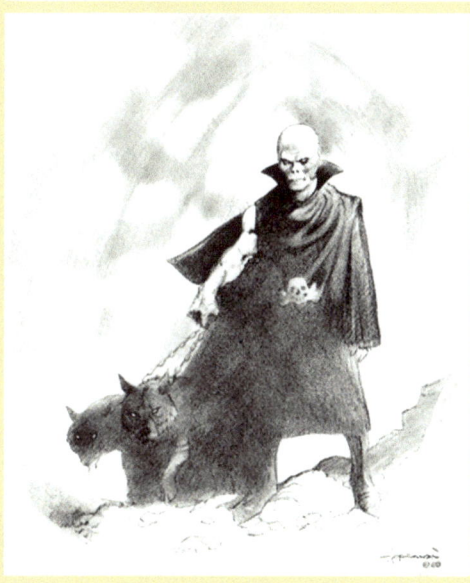

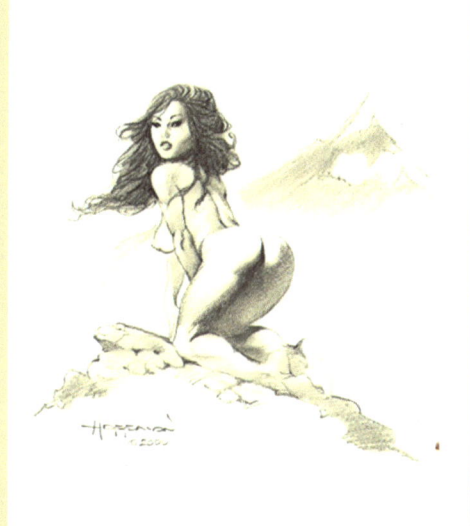

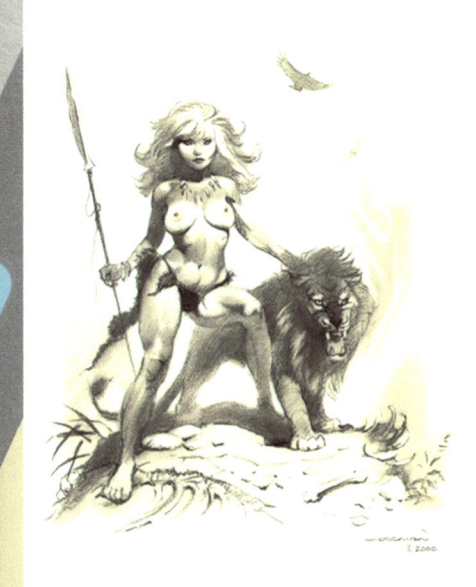

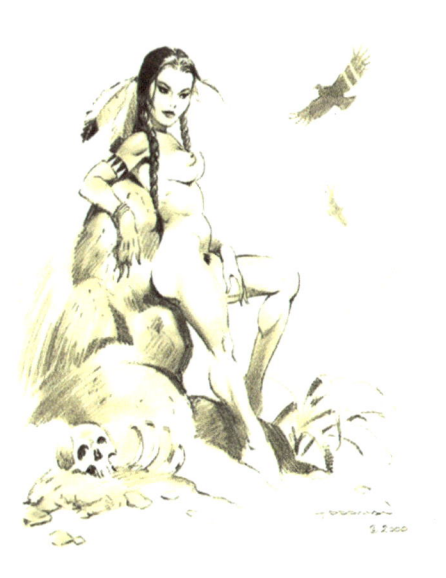

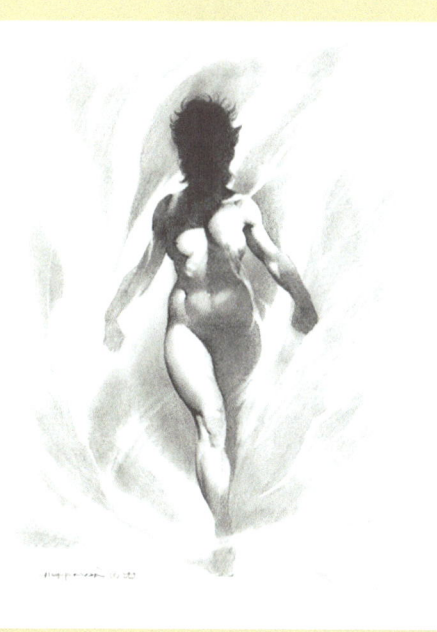

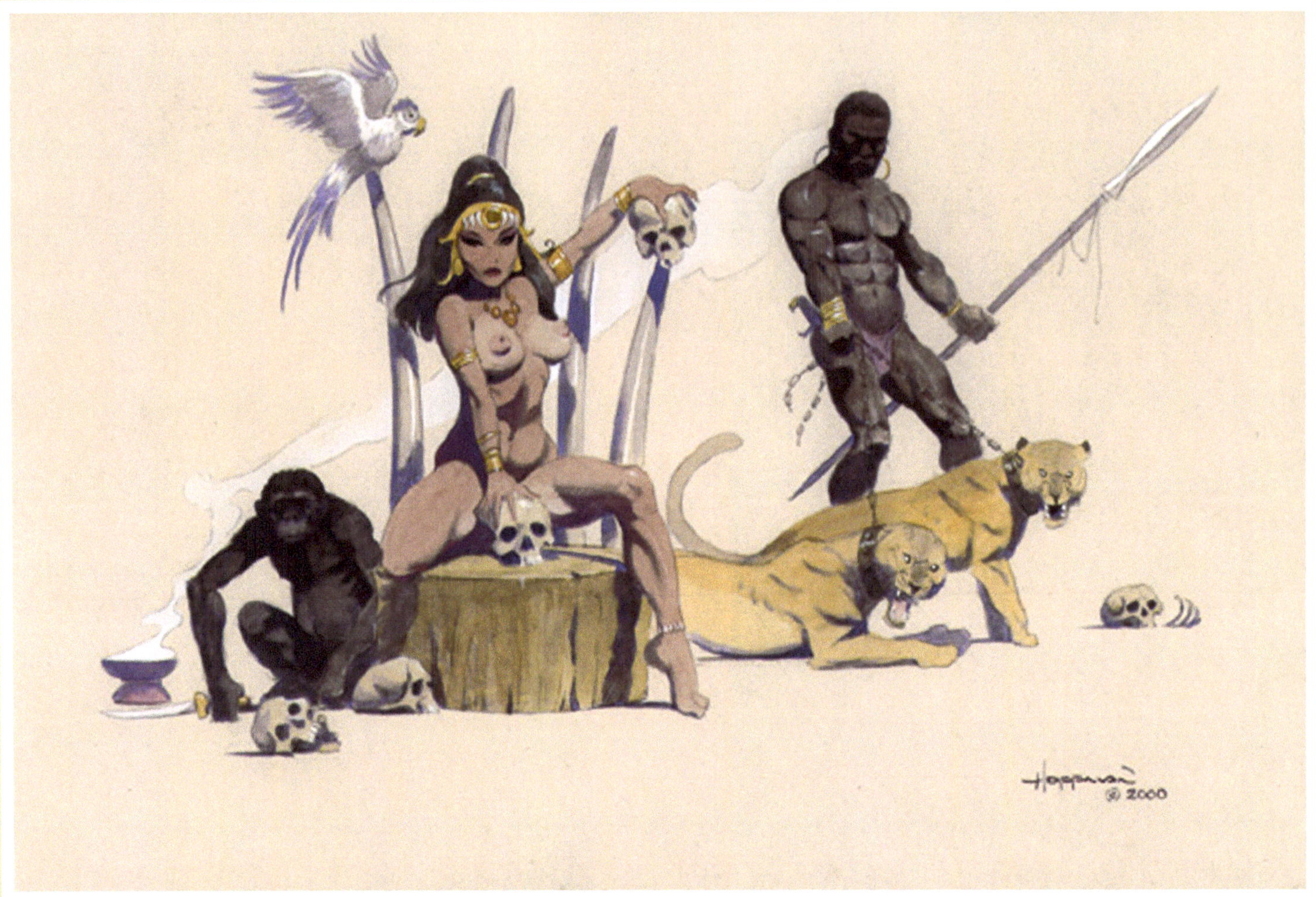

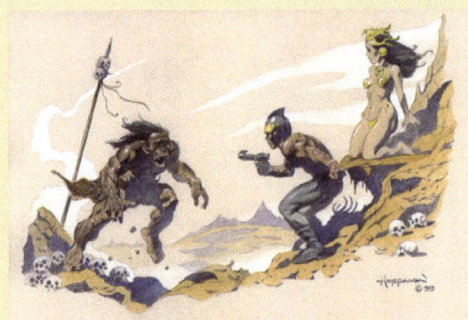
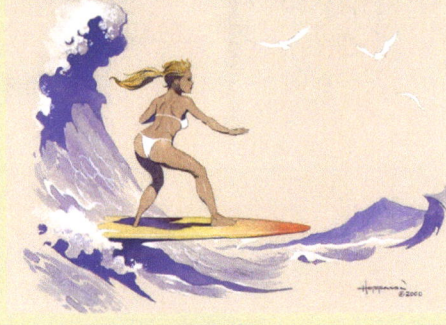
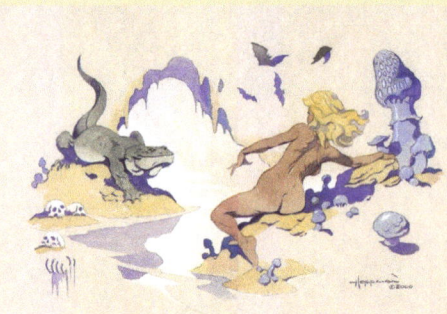
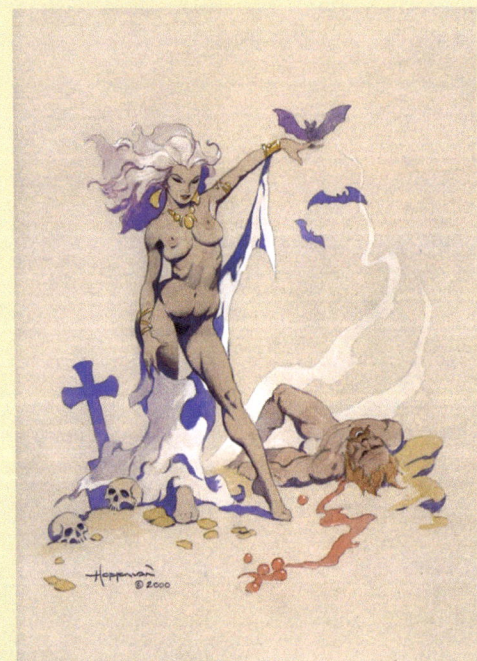
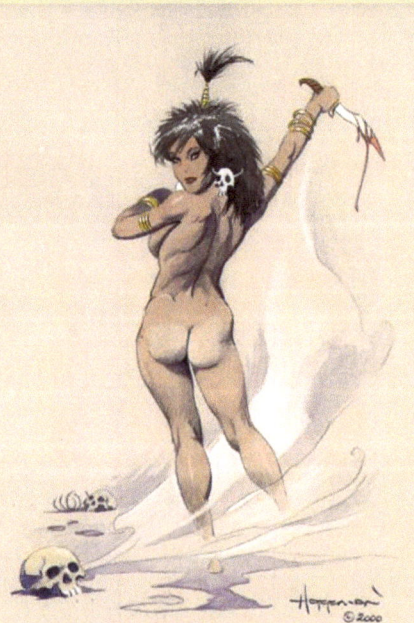
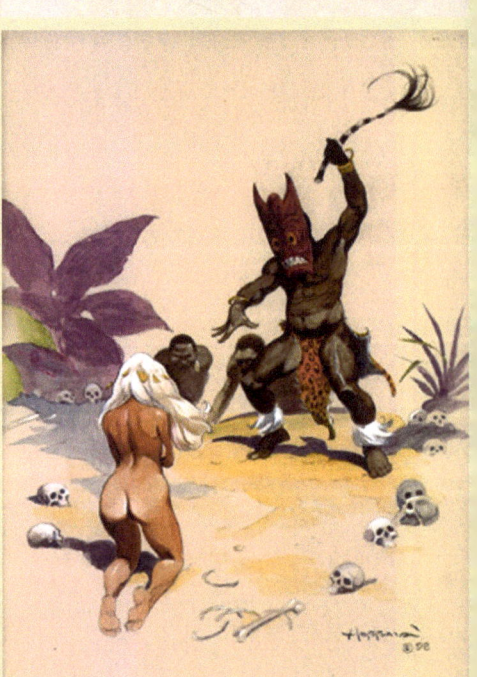

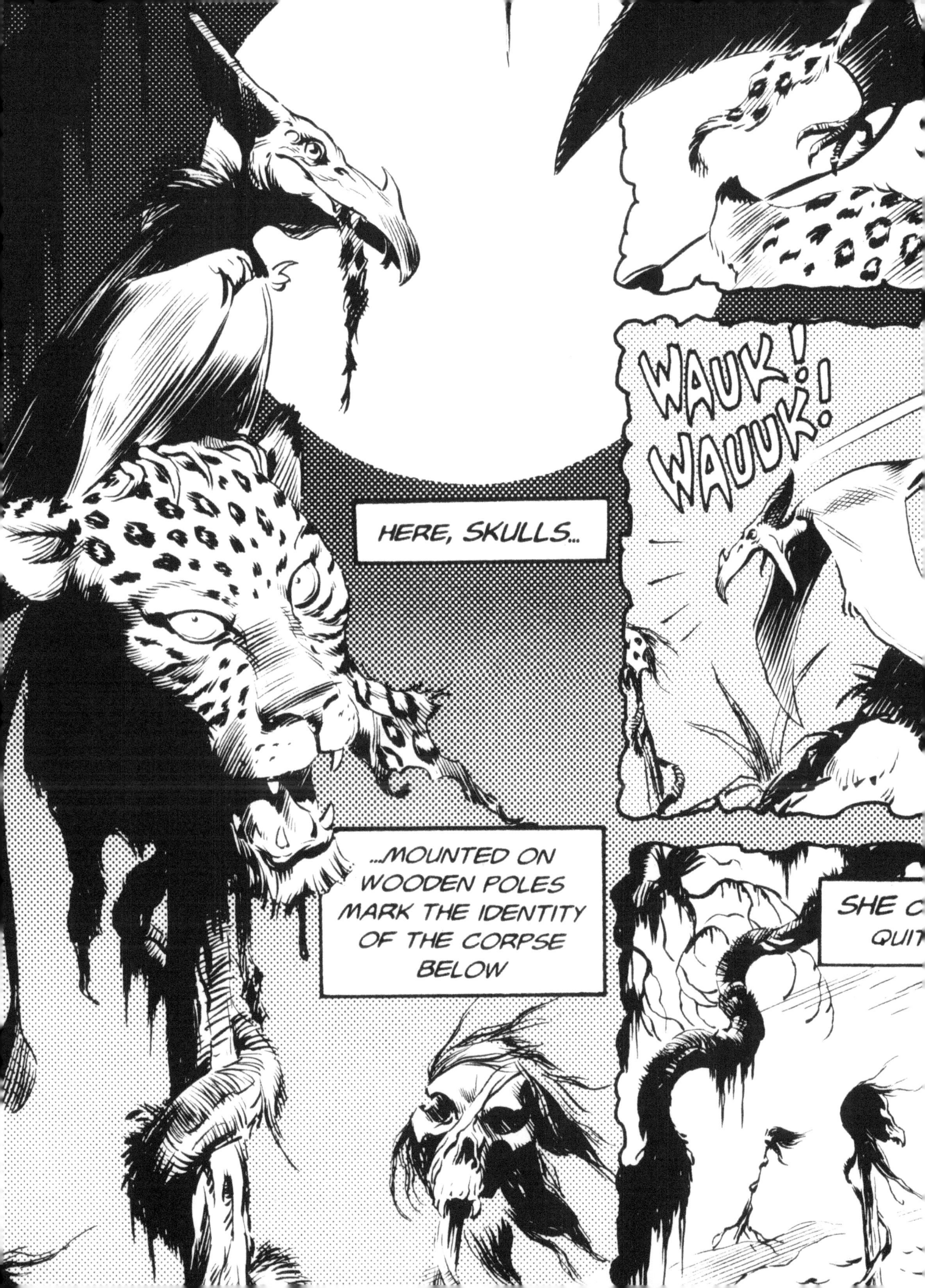

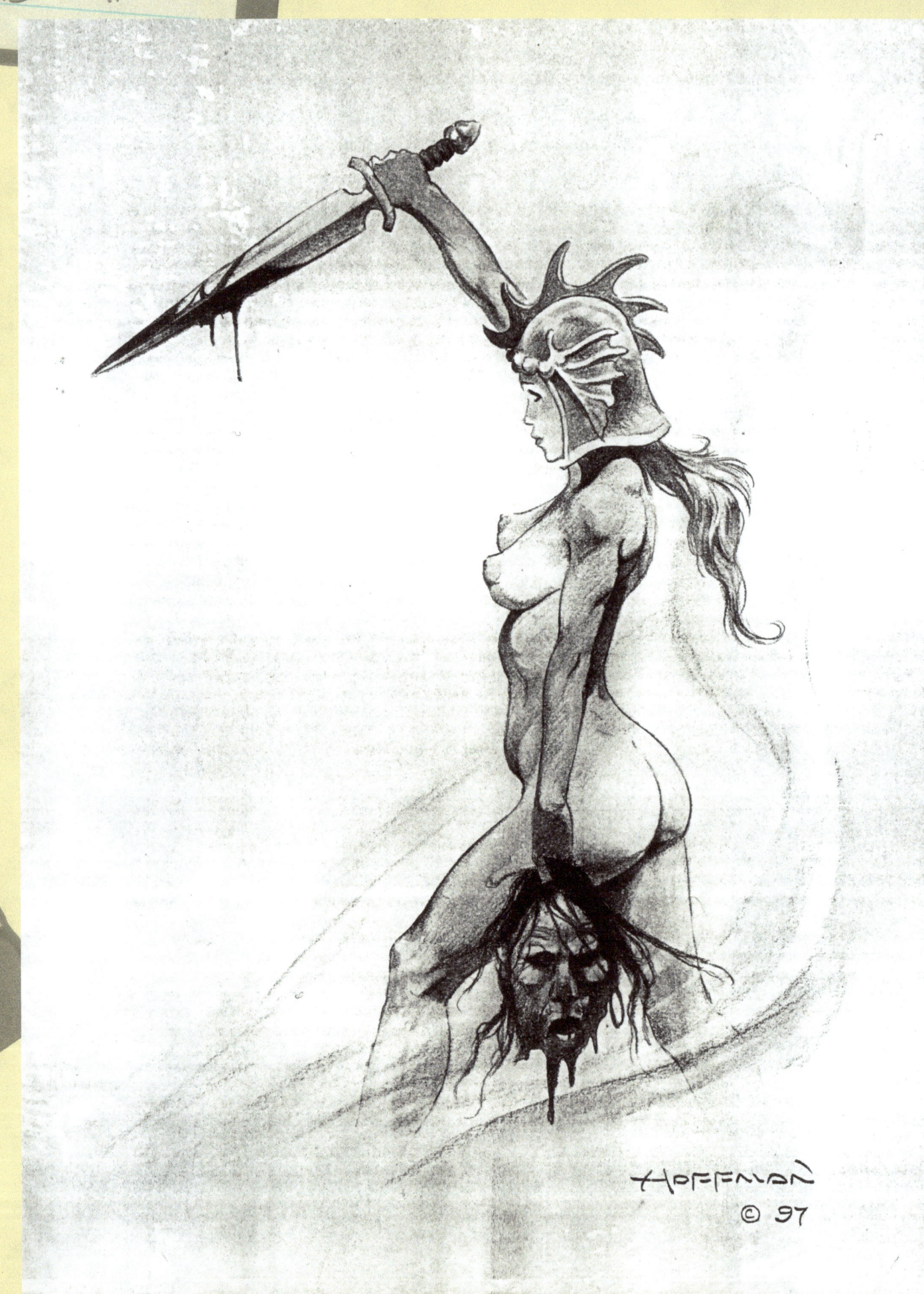

Comic book artists of that bygone age relied on the mythical "Zeer-Ox" to reproduce their work for transit on the legs of pigeons.

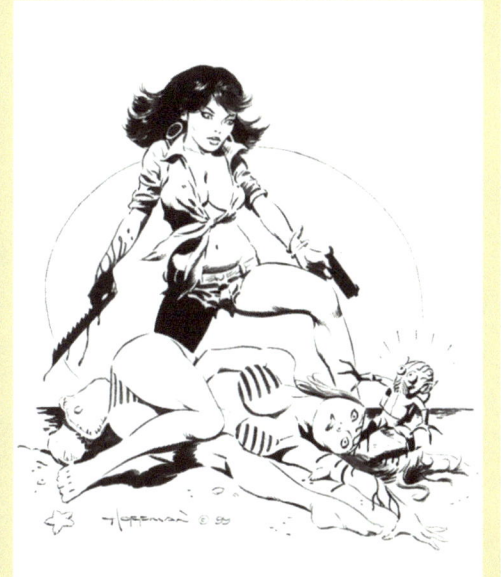

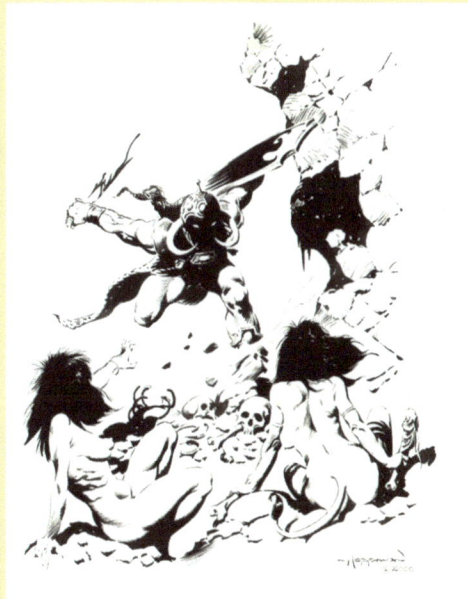

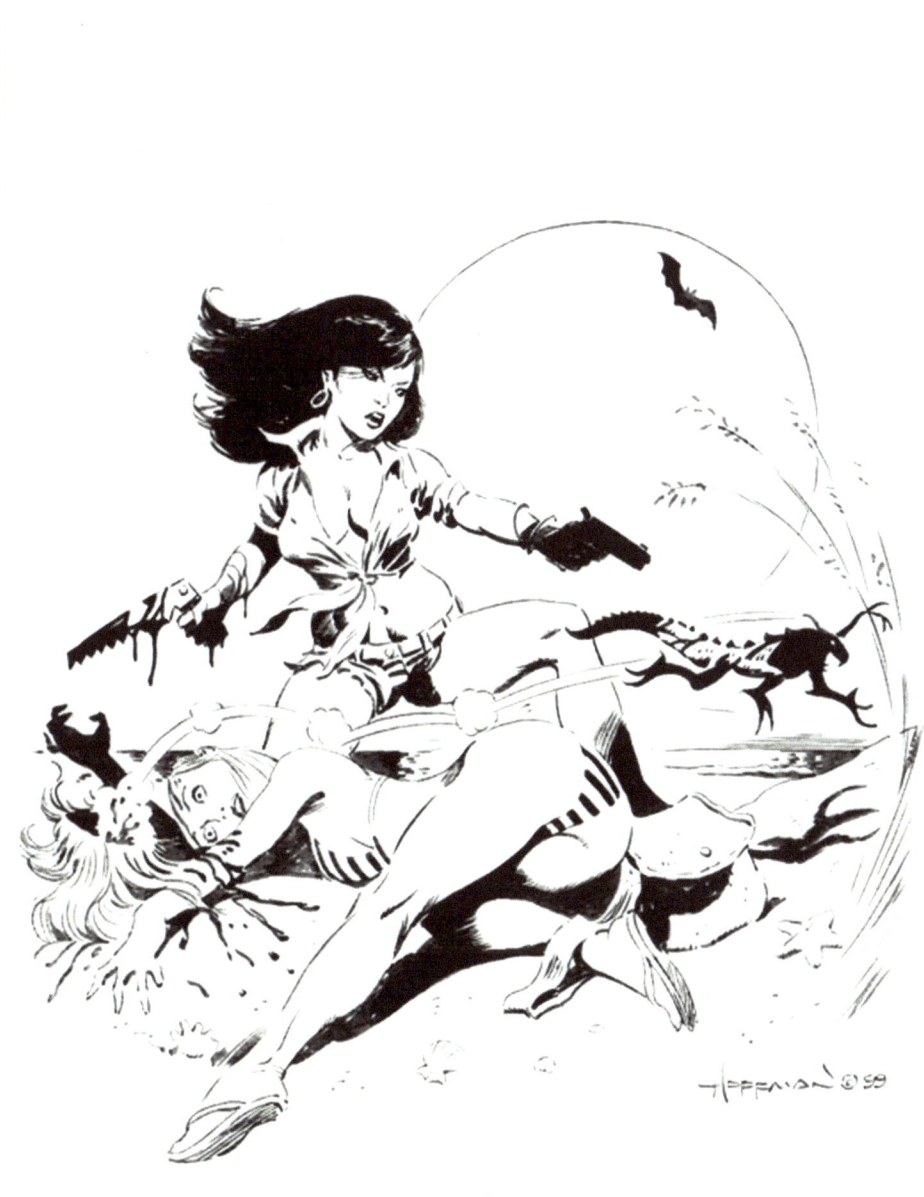

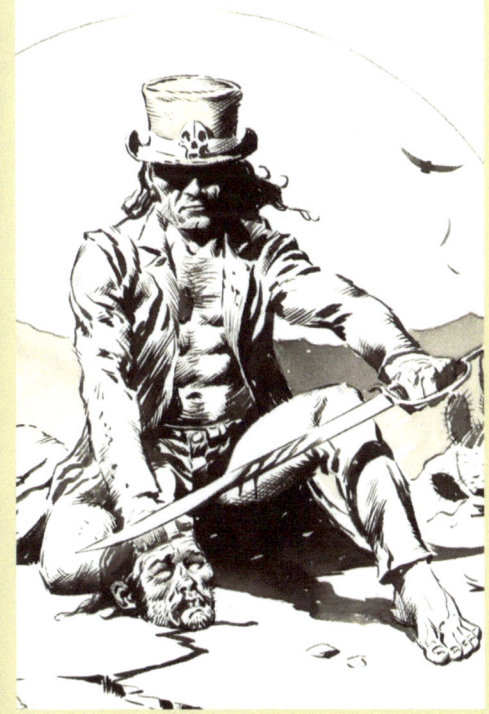

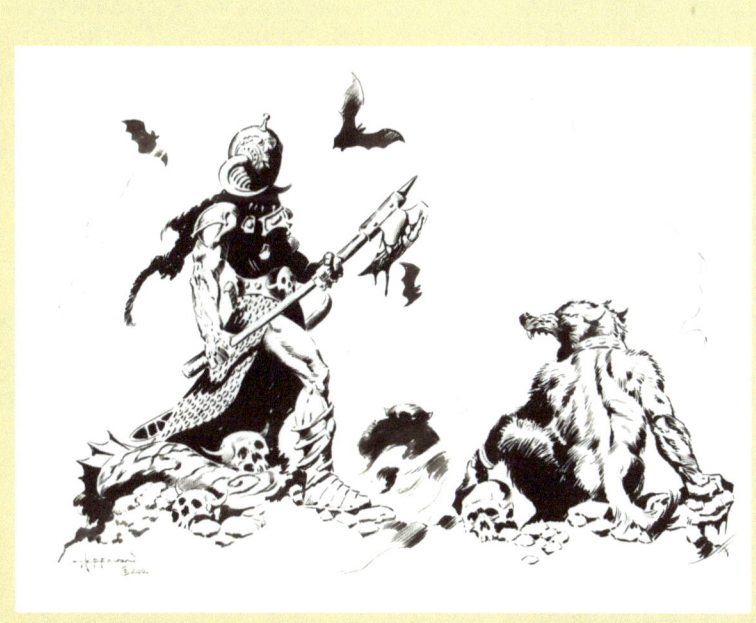

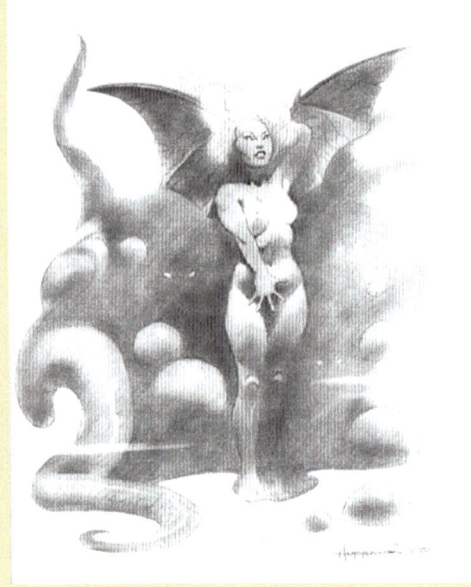

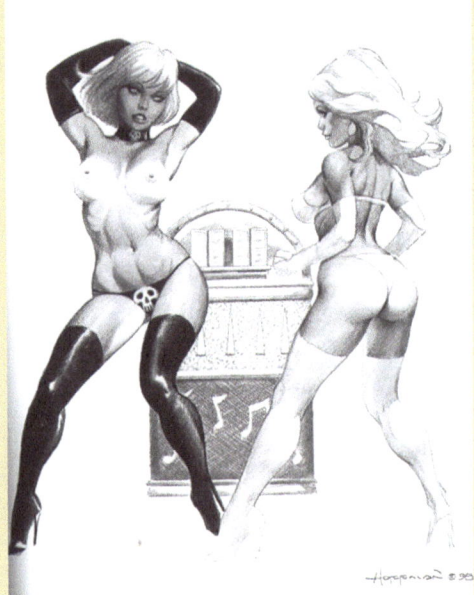

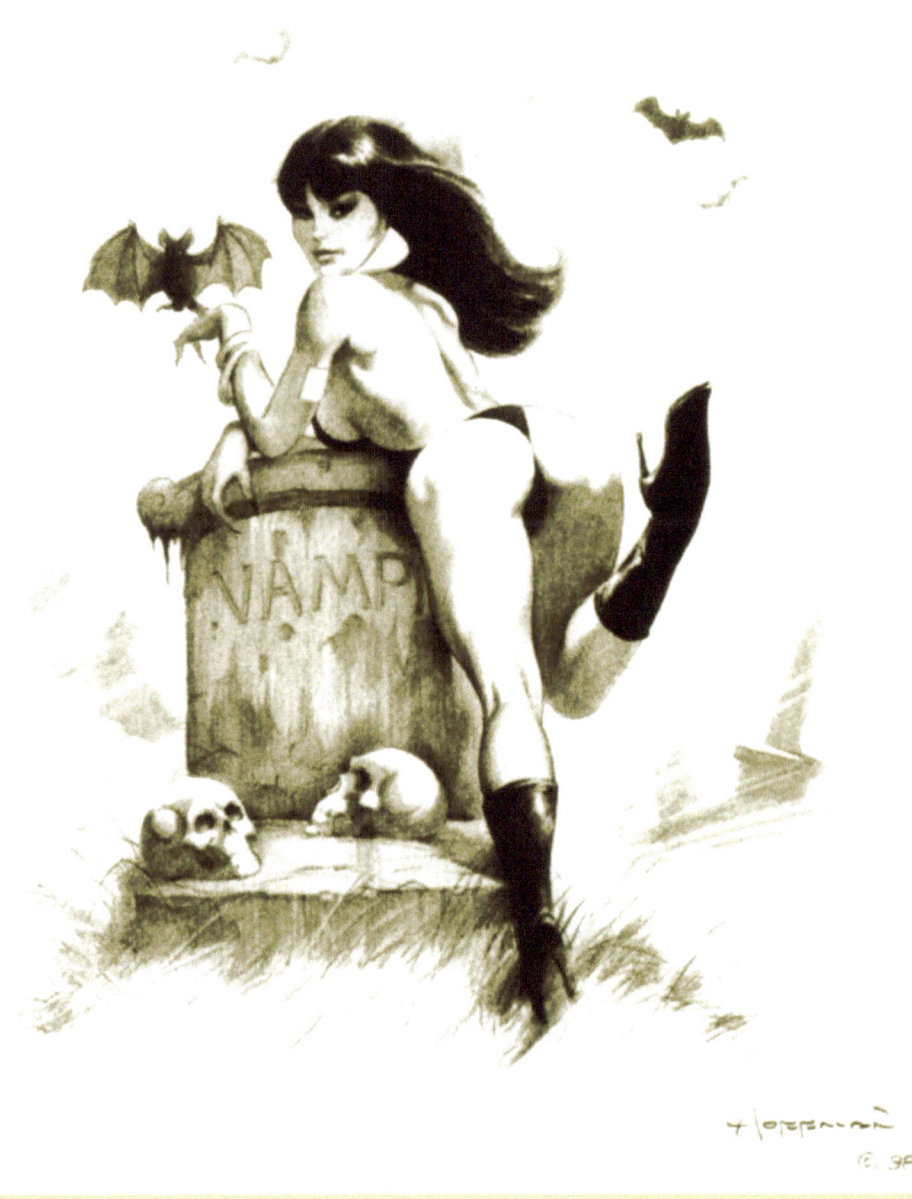

Hundreds of pencil drawings emerged to fill my quota in SQPs soft-core "art" books called the "Gallery Girls" series. In spite of the subject matter, room was made for less overtly sexual images like *Alien Wildlife* at bottom right. Then counterclockwise: *Biker Trash, Alice and Caterpillar, Jukebox, Batwing Girl,* and *Vampirella.*

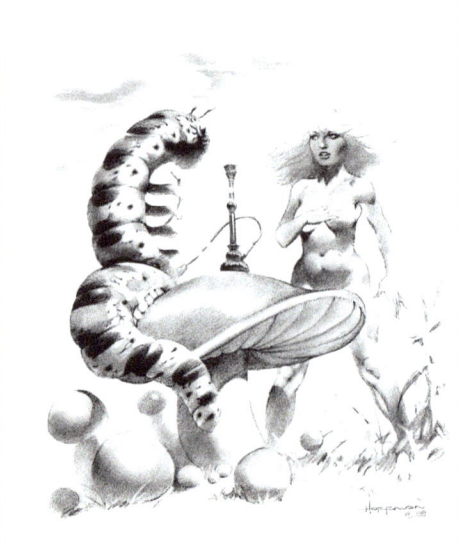

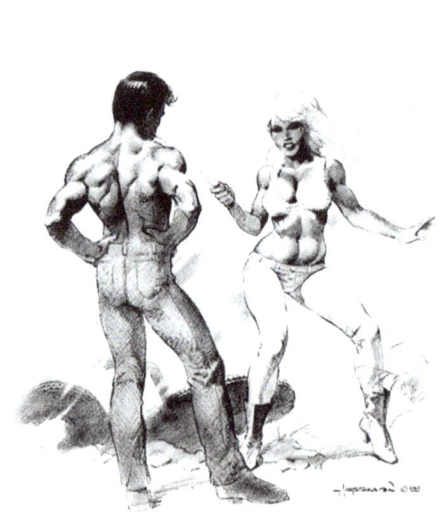

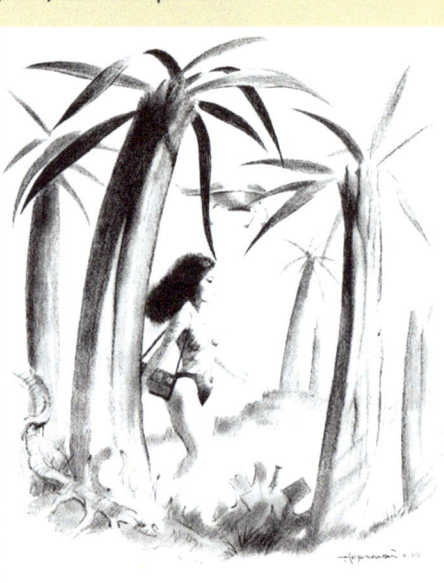

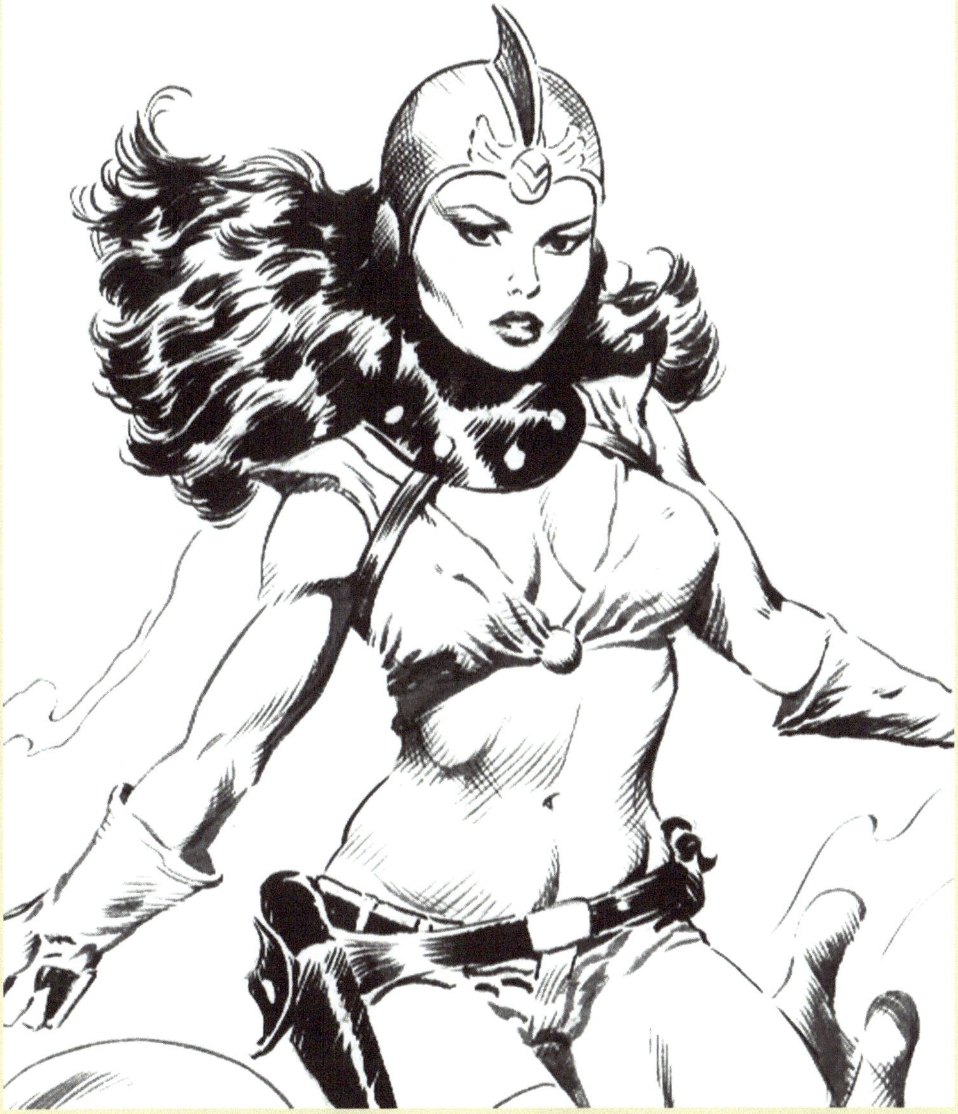

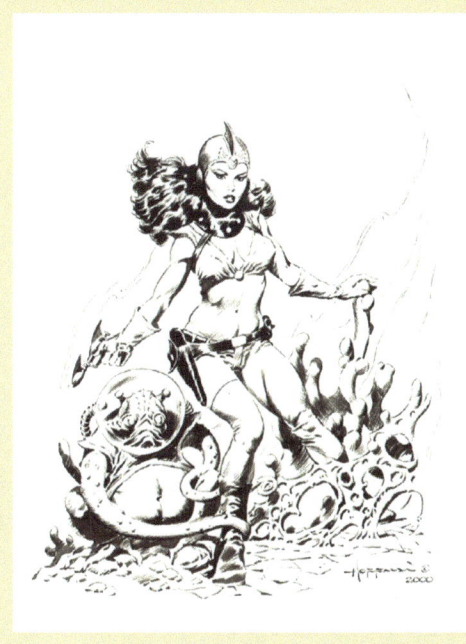

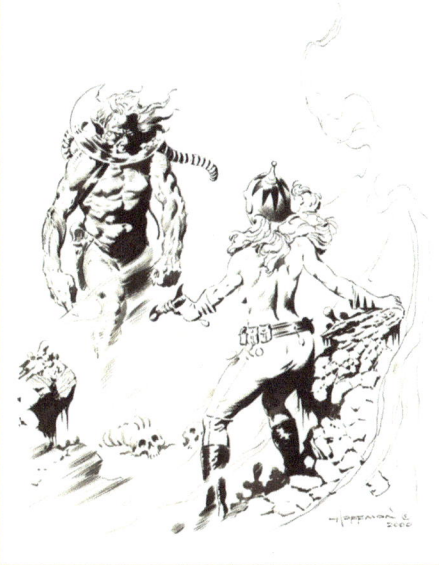

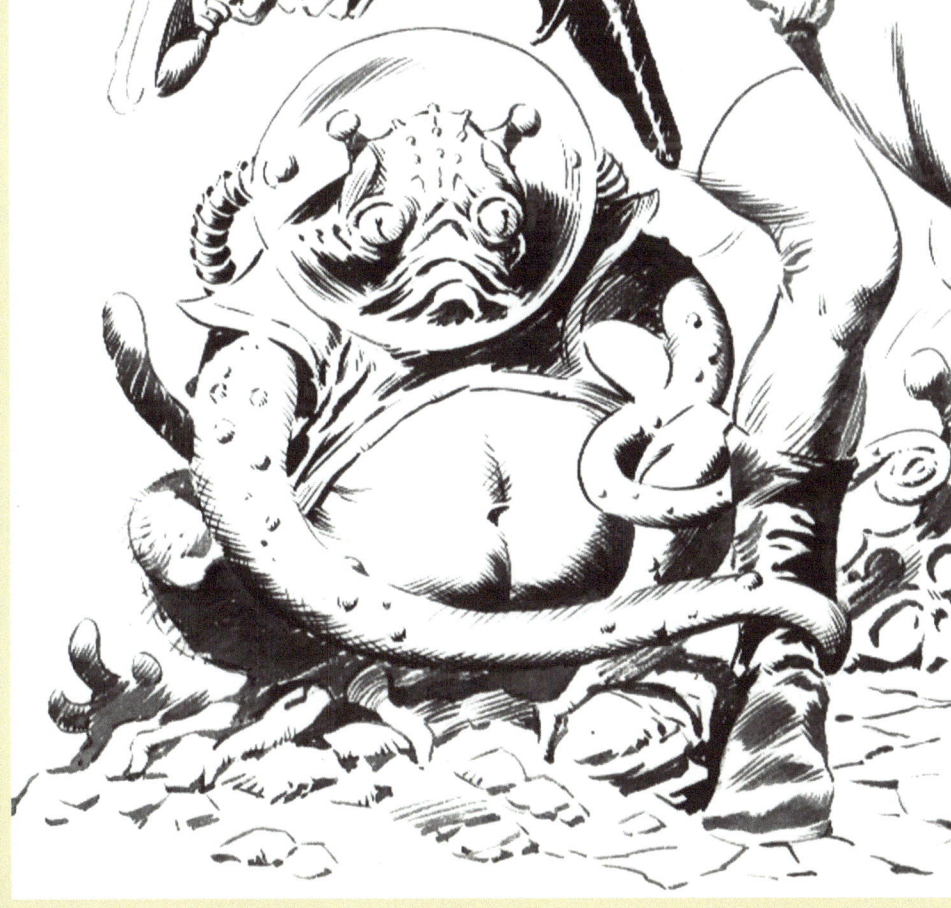

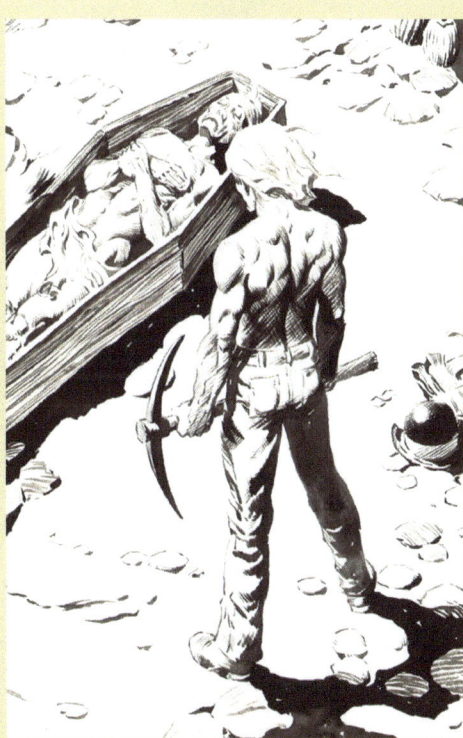

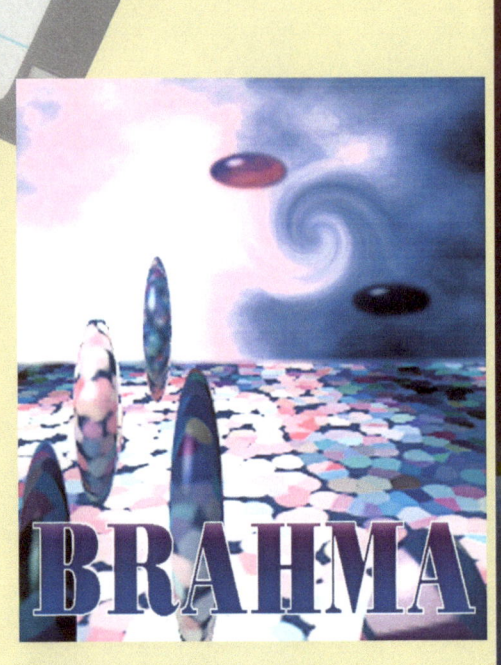

BRAHMA

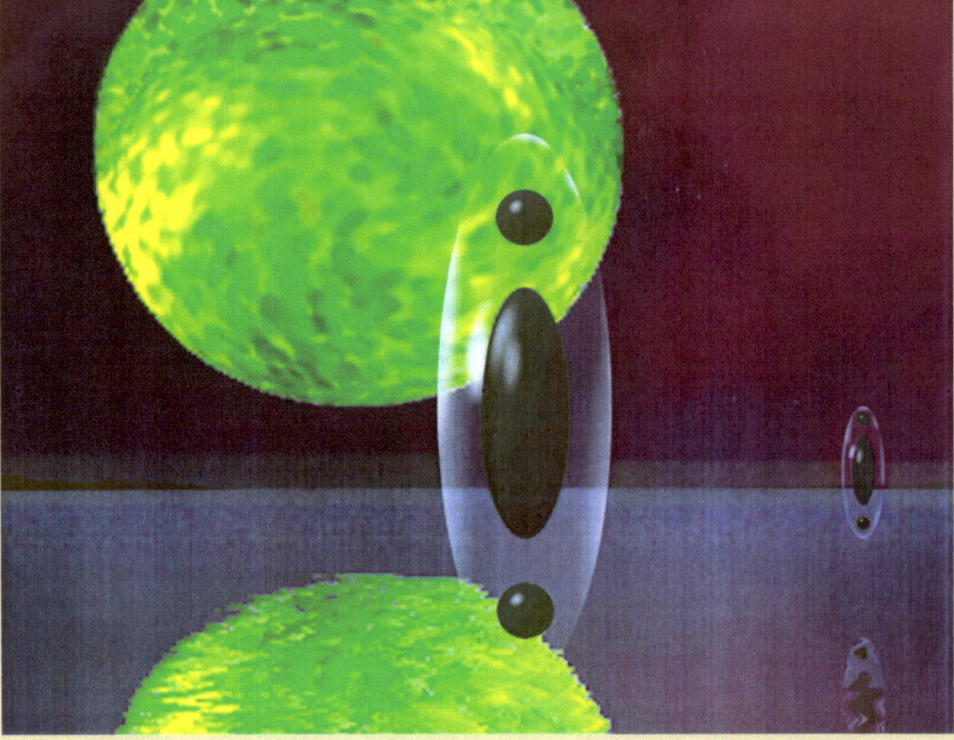

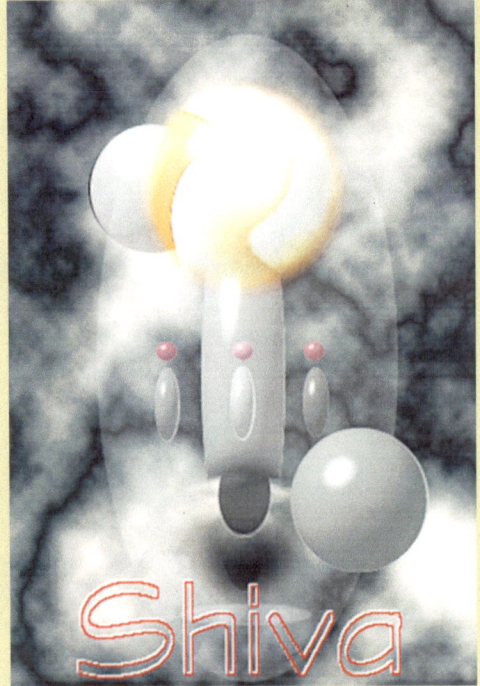

Shiva

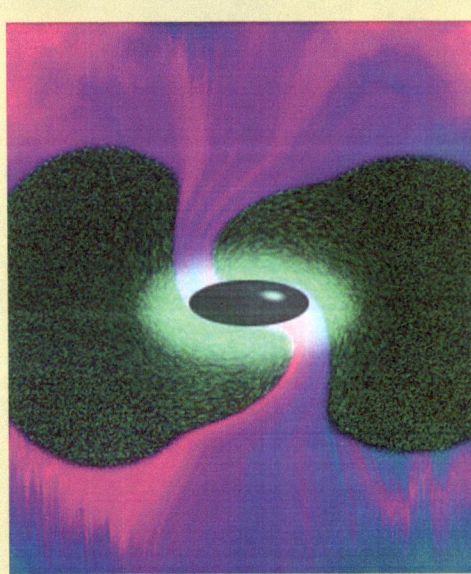

Was there any such thing as "Digital Art" way back in 1997? There was certainly a lot of talk--often worry--about the ramifications of computers on art, and implications about the replaceability of human creativity, as is often the case with the introduction of new technologies.

Today, approximately twelve years later, we're inundated and overwhelmed with so-called "Digital Art" at every turn; the common consensus now is that almost any kid with Photoshop and some other programs is somehow a full-fledged "artist", adept at creating complex, three dimen-sional scenes that are impressive and yet somehow false at the same time.

The art on these pages was created with a fairly creaking version of Photoshop 3.0, which today is beyond obsolete; nonethe-less, I find myself missing its "glass lens soft" feature, used extensively here to create these dimensional, rounded globes and ovaloids.

Above: *Green World,* a hypothetical alien world with enigmatic, hovering ellipsoids; top left and center: *Brahma* and *Shiva,* more intentionally incomprehensible alien ma-chineries; bottom: *Singularity* and *Sentinels.*

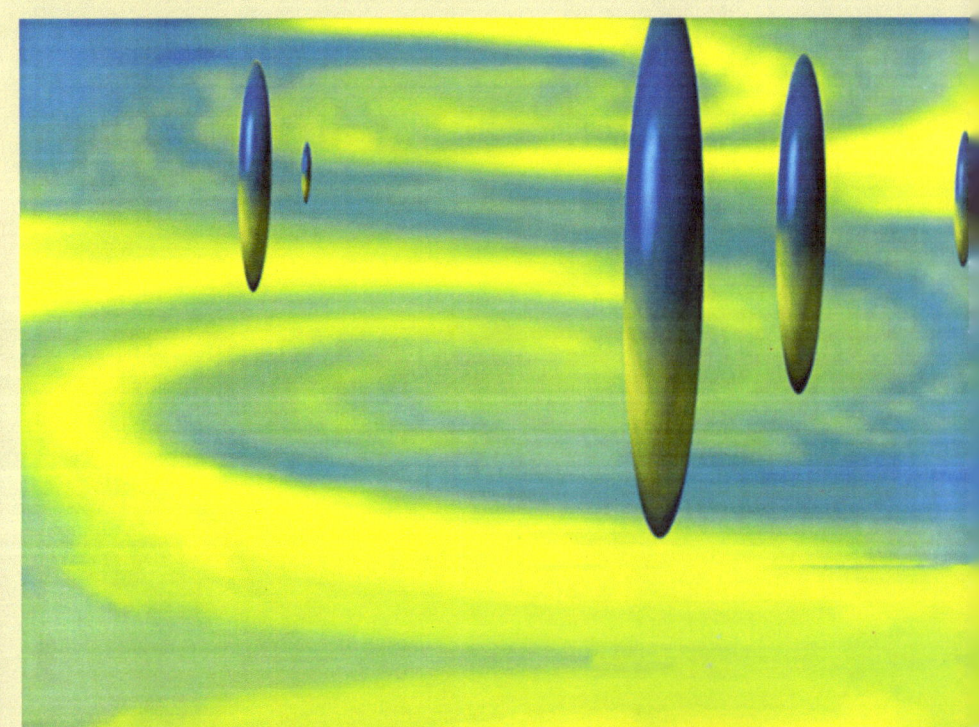

Experiments with the then-primitive computer graphics continued with pieces collaged from magazine clippings, like *Freefall,* right, depicting a band of futuristic, vehicleless travellers encountering "Shiva" on a distant world; I imagined a deafening machine noise given off by the enigmatic entity.

Below *Freefall* is *Station Girl;* I collaged two photographs together, one of an inverted airport, and I drew in the two robot figures in the upper right corner. The tortoiseshell object at left was meant to imply some sort of non-human intelligence.

Bottom right is *Near Planet,* a play of color as much as anything; bottom left is *Neighbors,* based on an obscure 1960s Japanese SF story which involved a robot apartment building and a protagonist interrupted while submerged in his tank of liquid; center left is *Rocket Rump,* painstakingly and completely drawn with a mouse.

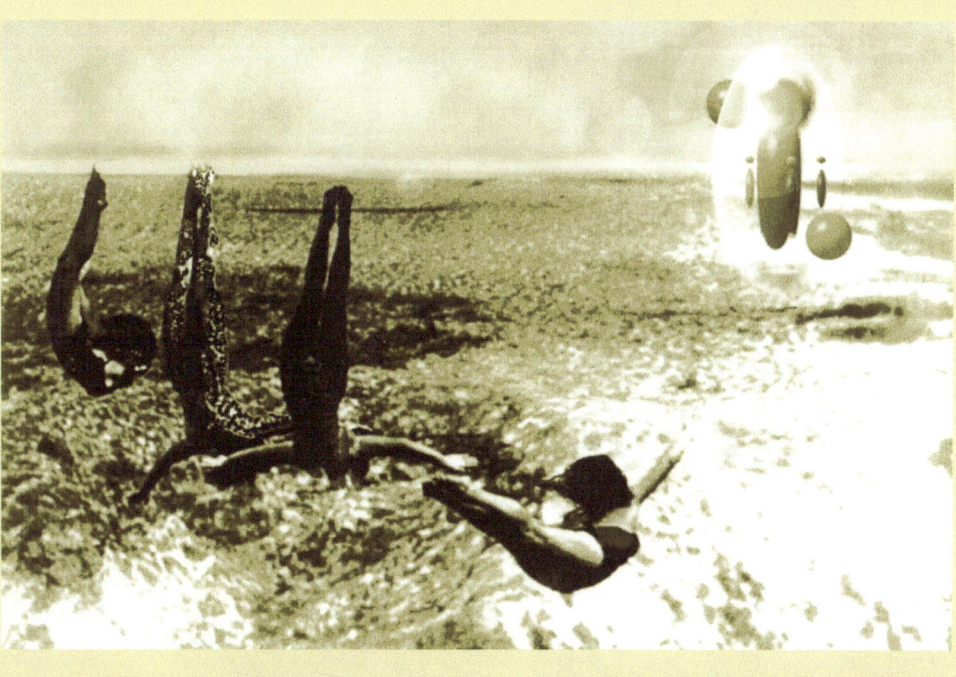

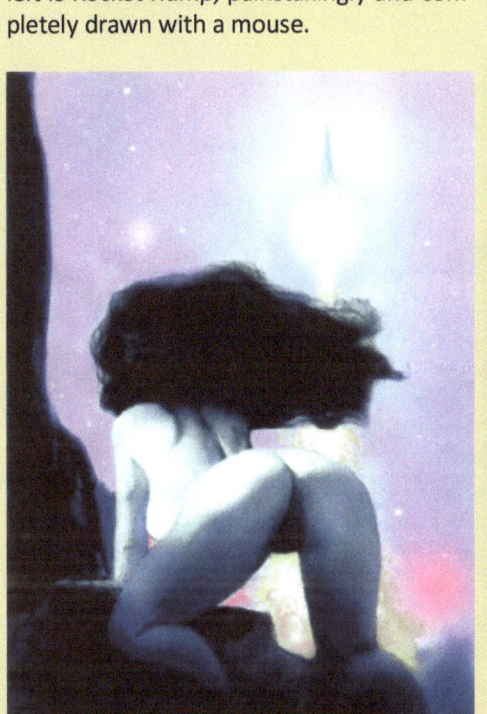

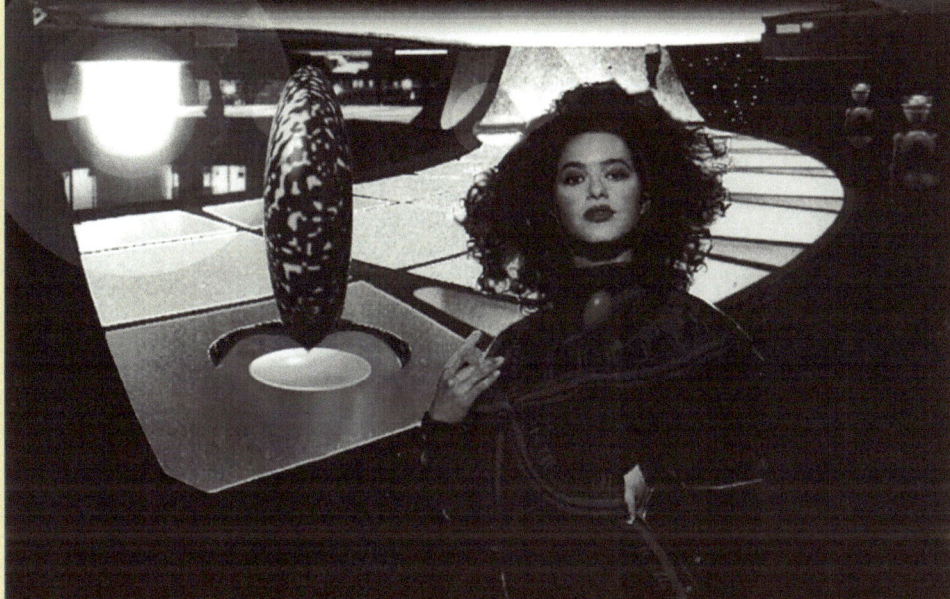

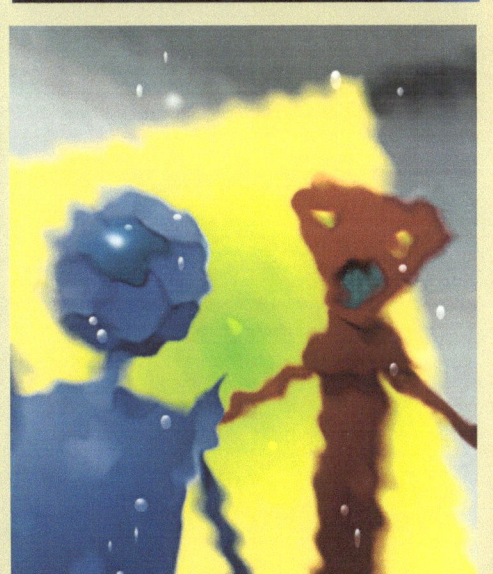

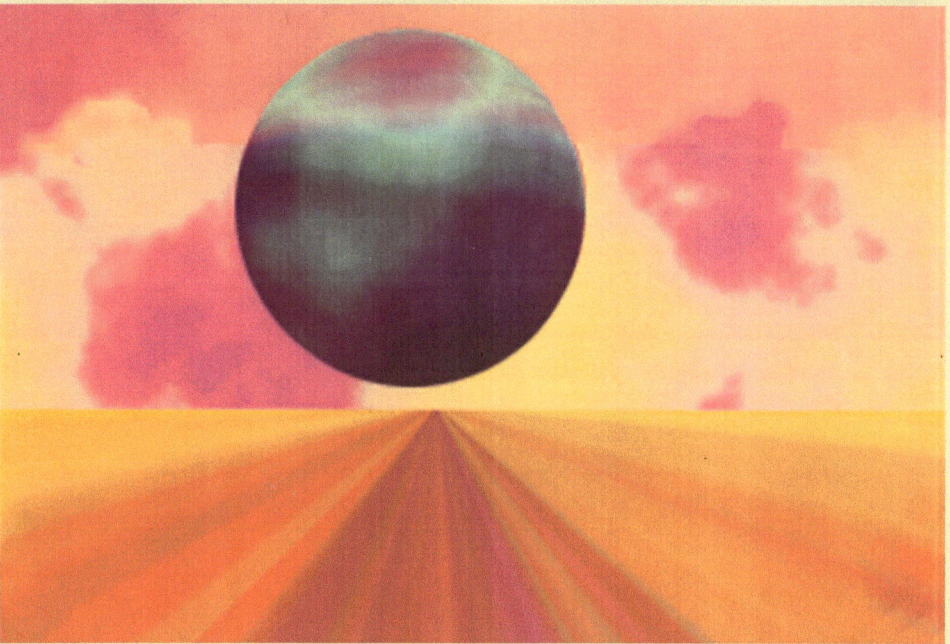

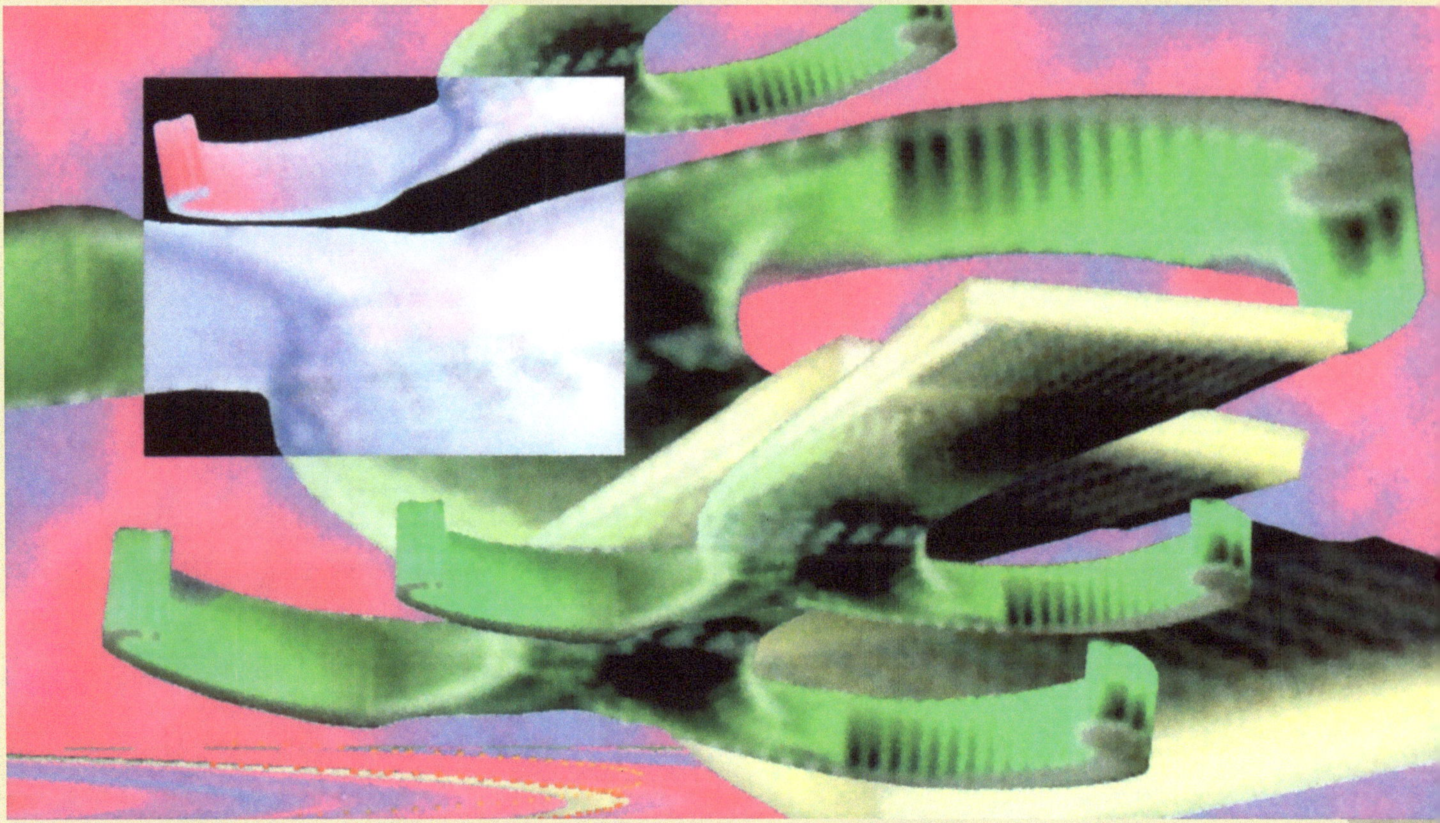

More early digital art: *Silicon Life,* top, created from collaged medical magazines, and from mathematical patterns: *Rigel Powergrid.*

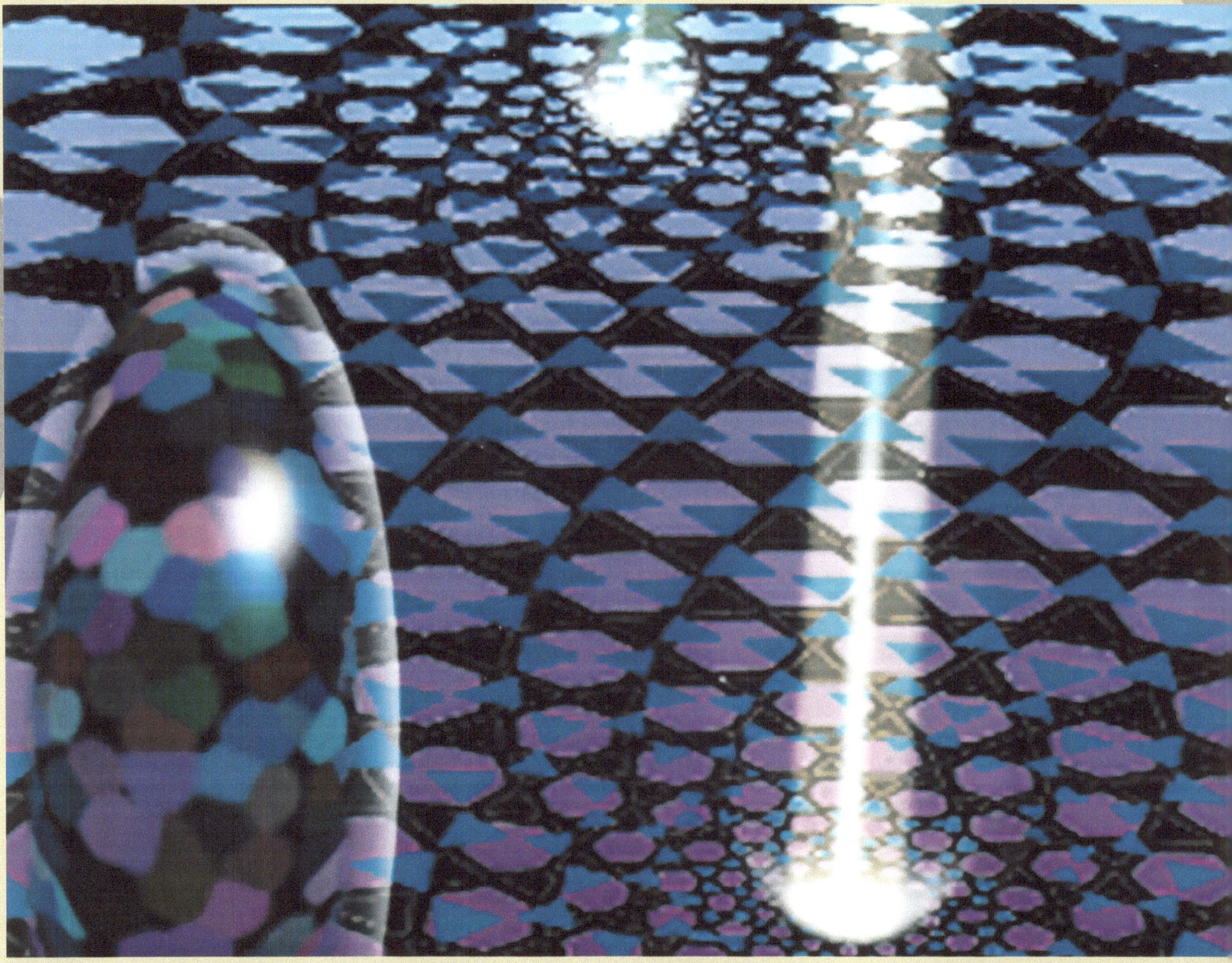

www.ingramcontent.com/pod-product-compliance
Lightning Source LLC
Chambersburg PA
CBHW040752200526
45159CB00025B/1862